CAVE OF THE WINDS.

"Dread awe-inspiring Cavern! 'Mong the New,
Wild, Wondrous objects that around I view,
None strikes the soul like thee! Thou seem'st to me
The very portal of sublimity!
And Nature—as if dreading to expose
The hidden mysteries of her mighty throes—
Hath thrown over thee a wide spread, beautious veil,
Woven from the air-hung waters—snatched from out
Their wonted channel for this strong avail—
And dyed it with the loveliest tints throughout—
E'en fringed it with a rainbow!"

THIS WONDERFUL CAVE
IS UNDER
Center Fall & Luna Island

It was discovered a few years since by J. W Ingraham, Esq., who gave it its present name. It was first entered by Mr. G. W. Sims, and Mr. B. H. White of Niagara Falls, it was then a most hazardous and difficult undertaking; yet they acknowledged themselves fully rewarded in the new and magnificent scene which this lofty cavern presented.—Since then, until the last two years, few have ventured into it. But its safety can no longer be doubted. A wall has been built above, and rocks excavated below, so that it is now quite easy of access.

The subscriber would inform those who wish to visit this Cavern, that they have erected a dressing room under the bank, have furnished it with dresses suitable, and have put down a firm ladder into the mouth of the Cave, and are prepared to guide persons behind this sheet of water into the Cave with perfect ease and safety.

☞ For further particulars, enquire of the subscribers, at the Cataract House.

S. HOOKER & SON, Guides to the Falls.

Niagara Falls, May, 1850.

RALPH GREENHILL & THOMAS D. MAHONEY

NIAGARA

UNIVERSITY OF TORONTO PRESS

PRINTED IN CANADA
SBN 8020-1565-4

This book
was designed by
LAURIE LEWIS
under the direction of
ALLAN FLEMING
of the
University of
Toronto
Press

CONTENTS

Preface
vii

The Image
1

Frontier
25

Expansion
57

Stunters
81

Tourists
109

Power
153

Bibliography and Index
177

The advertisements on the endpapers
are reproduced from
New guide book of Niagara Falls for strangers
by George H. Hackstaff.
This guide-book was printed in 1850
at Hackstaff's newspaper office in Niagara Falls, N.Y.
These advertisements,
and all other illustrations not otherwise credited,
are from the collections of the authors.

PREFACE

This book grew out of a joint interest in the iconography and history of Niagara. Our concern, however, is not primarily with local history, but with those aspects of Niagara that have made an impact on North America and, at times, the whole western world. By 1900 the significant developments had taken place, and we have, therefore, virtually excluded twentieth-century events from the six essays dealing with different aspects of Niagara's history.

We are most grateful to the institutions that allowed us to reproduce pictures and other material from their collections. We are particularly indebted to Mrs Mary Allodi of the Royal Ontario Museum, Alan Fern of the Library of Congress, Robert M. Vogel of the Smithsonian Institution, and Ruth Witmer of the Public Library, Niagara Falls, N.Y. for their friendly help and interest in our project. Several fellow-collectors – Mrs Lorraine Dexter, J. Stuart Fleming, Frederick S. Lightfoot, Mrs Lura Woodside Watkins, and Paul Wing, Jr. – greatly assisted us, and in our search for material we were also fortunate to have had the help of Mrs Anne P. Brennan, Craig Ross, and Dana Tillou. Finally we should like to acknowledge our indebtedness to Verschoyle Benson Blake for his advice, criticism, and encouragement.

RG

TDM

THE IMAGE

The first eye-witness description of Niagara was written by Father Louis Hennepin, a Recollect priest from the Spanish Netherlands. In *Description de la Louisiane*, published in 1683, he gave a brief account of the 'incredible Cataract or Waterfall, which has no equal'. Hennepin had been one of the first white men to see the Falls, which he visited in the winter of 1678-79 when serving as a missionary under La Salle. In 1697, ten years after La Salle's death, Hennepin's book, *Nouvelle decouverte d'un tres grand pays situé dans l'Amerique*, was published at Utrecht with a fulsome dedication to William III of England, who as Prince of Orange had become an ally of Spain in the defence of the Netherlands. The first English translation was published in London the following year, with the title *A new discovery of a vast country in America*. In this book, Hennepin appropriated an account of La Salle's expedition to the mouth of the Mississippi, and greatly enlarged his original description of Niagara.

'Betwixt the Lake *Ontario* and *Eriè*, there is a vast and prodigious Cadence of Water which falls down after a surprizing and astonishing manner, insomuch that the Universe does not afford its Parallel. 'Tis true, *Italy* and *Suedeland* boast of some such Things; but we may well say they are but sorry Patterns, when compar'd to this of which we now speak. At the foot of this horrible Precipice, we meet with the River *Niagara*, which is not above a quarter of a League broad, but is wonderfully deep in some places. It is so rapid above this Descent, that it violently hurries down the wild Beasts while endeavouring to pass it to feed on the other side, they not being able to withstand the force of its Current, which inevitably casts them headlong above Six hundred foot high.

'This wonderful Downfal, is compounded of two great Cross-streams of Water, and two Falls, with an Isle sloping along the middle of it. The Waters which fall from this horrible Precipice, do foam and boyl after the most hideous manner imaginable, making an outrageous Noise, more terrible than that of Thunder; for when the Wind blows out of the South, their dismal roaring may be heard more than Fifteen Leagues off.

'The River *Niagara* having thrown itself down this incredible Precepice, continues its impetuous course for two Leagues together, to the great Rock abovemention'd [Queenston Heights], with an inexpressible rapidity: But having past that, its impetuousity relents, gliding along more gently for other two Leagues, till it arrive at the Lake *Ontario* or *Frontenac*.'

The *Nouvelle decouverte* and its English translation were the first books to include a picture of the Falls – an imaginative engraving. This largely fantastic picture was copied in numerous prints of the eighteenth century. It also became the basis of other engravings, and versions of it appear as late as the 1830s. In fact, the 'Hennepin' view became not only the European image of Niagara, but a symbol of America itself.

Another famous early traveller, Baron de Lahontan, visited the Falls in 1688. The very popular account of his travels added to the exaggerations of Hennepin: 'As for the Waterfall of *Niagara*; 'tis seven or eight hundred foot high, and half a League broad.' Eighteenth-century geographies repeated these exaggerations, even though in 1721 Charlevoix, the best known of the early Jesuit writers on America, wrote in a letter from the Falls that he 'found the baron de la Hontan had committed such a mistake with respect to its height and figure, as to give grounds to believe he had never seen it ... For my own part, after having examined it on all sides, where it could be viewed to the greatest advantage, I am inclined to think we cannot allow it less than a hundred and forty, or fifty feet.'

The true height of the Falls continued to be a matter of considerable concern to the early travellers. In 1750, Peter Kalm, the Swedish botanist, wrote to a friend in Philadelphia: 'I doubt not but you have a desire to learn the exact height of this great fall. Father *Hennepin*, you know, calls it 600 feet perpendicular; but he has gain'd little credit in *Canada*; the name of honour they give him there, is *un grand Menteur*, or *the great Liar*; he writes of what he saw in places where he never was. 'Tis true he saw this fall: But as it is the way of some travellers to magnify every thing, so has he done with regard to the fall of *Niagara* ... Since Father *Hennepin*'s time, this fall, in all the accounts that have been given of it, has grown less and less; and those who have measur'd it with mathematical instruments find the perpendicular fall of the water to be exactly 137 feet.'

Kalm's figure of 137 feet was in the old French measurement and was equivalent to about 146 English feet. Similarly Charlevoix's estimate was about 150 to 160 feet in our measurement. One hundred and sixty feet has generally been accepted as being the height of the Falls, before the diversion of half the water of the Niagara River for power purposes in the twentieth century. This diversion has had the effect of reducing the level of the pool below the Falls by about twenty feet, and thereby increasing the height by about the same amount.

The noise of the Falls was also a subject of great controversy. Peter Kalm disputed Hennepin here too: 'You may remember, to what great distance *Hennepin* says the noise of this fall may be heard. All the gentlemen who were with me, agreed, that the farthest one can hear it, is 15 leagues, and that very seldom ... Sometimes, 'tis said, the fall makes a much greater noise than at other times; and this is look'd on as a certain mark of approaching bad weather, or rain; the *Indians* here hold it always for a sure sign. When I was there, it did not make an extraordinary great noise: Just by the fall, we could easily hear what each other said, without speaking much louder than common when conversing in other places. I do not know how others found so great a noise here; perhaps it was at certain times, as abovementioned.' Kalm's letter was first published in January 1751 in the *Gentleman's Magazine* – which was illustrated the following month, most inappropriately, with an engraving copied from the 'Hennepin' picture.

The earliest known true pictures of the Falls, and certainly among the most beautiful that have ever been painted of Niagara, are the two watercolours by Thomas Davies, now in the possession of the New-York Historical Society. Davies had come to North America in 1758 as a 'Lieutenant of Fireworks' in the Royal Artillery. Like other British officers he had been trained in topographical drawing, and spent much of his spare time painting extraordinarily vivid pictures of the country. A drawing of Niagara by Davies and a sketch by a fellow-officer in the Royal Artillery, Lieutenant William Pierie, were published as engravings, but it was not until after the American Revolution, when Niagara became less remote and inaccessible, that such engravings made from the realistic sketches of various travellers began to supplant the many versions of the 'Hennepin'.

Travellers in the latter half of the eighteenth century wrote mainly matter-of-fact accounts of the Falls. 'As these have been visited by so many travellers, and so frequently described," wrote Captain Jonathan Carver in his *Travels through the interior parts of North-America, in the years 1766, 1767, and 1768*, 'I shall omit giving a particular description of them, and only observe, that the waters by which they are supplied, after taking their rise near two thousand miles to the north-west, and passing through the Lakes Superior, Michegan, Huron, and Erie, during which they have been receiving constant accumulations, at length rush down a stupendous precipice of one hundred and forty feet perpendicular; and in a strong rapid, that extends to the distance of eight or nine miles below, fall nearly as much more: this River soon after empties itself into Lake Ontario.'

The nineteenth-century visitors, on the other hand, often indulged themselves in effusive descriptions of their emotions. 'I have seen the Falls, and am all rapture and amazement', Thomas Moore, the Irish poet, wrote in a letter to his mother in 1804. 'Never shall I forget the impression I felt at the first glimpse of them which we got as the carriage passed over the hill that overlooks them. We were not near enough to be agitated by the terrific effects of the scene; but saw through the trees this mighty flow of waters descending with calm magnificence, and received enough of its grandeur to set imagination on the wing; imagination which, even at Niagara, can outrun reality. I felt as if approaching the very residence of the Deity; the tears started into my eyes; and I remained, for moments after we had lost sight of the scene, in that delicious absorption which pious enthusiasm alone can produce. We arrived at the New Ladder and descended to the bottom. Here all its awful sublimities rushed full upon me ... My whole heart and soul ascended towards the Divinity in a swell of devout admiration, which I never before experienced. Oh! bring the atheist here, and he cannot return an atheist! I pity the man who can coldly sit down to write a description of these ineffable wonders; much more do I pity him who can submit them to the admeasurement of gallons and yards. It is impossible by pen or pencil to convey even a faint idea of their magnificence. Painting is lifeless; and the most burning words of poetry have all been lavished upon inferior and ordinary subjects. We must have new combinations of language to describe the Falls of Niagara.'

Another Irishman, Tyrone Power, the actor, visited the Falls in 1836. The guide, who led him under the Horseshoe Falls to Termination Rock, had been a stable-hand at a friend's house in Ireland two years earlier.

' "Isn't it illegant, sir,?" began the "Conductor", as soon as we were well clear of the mist.

' "Isn't it a noble sight intirely? Caps the world for grandness any way, that's sartain!"

'I need hardly say that in this opinion we all joined loudly; but Mr. Conductor was not yet done with us, – he had now to give us a taste of his "larnin".

' "I wish ye'd take notice, sir," said he, pointing across the river with an air of authority and a look of infinite wisdom. "Only take a luk at the falls; an' you'll see that Shakspeare is out altogether about the description."

' "How's that, Pat?" inquired I, although not a little taken aback by the authority so gravely quoted by my critical friend.

' "Why, sir, Shakspeare first of all says that there's two falls; now, ye may see wid yer own eyes that it's one river sure, and one fall, only for the shtrip o' rock that makes two af id ..."

'Again I agreed with him, excusing Shakspeare's discrepancies on the score of his never having had a proper guide to explain these matters.

' "I don't know who at all showed him the place," gravely responded Pat; "but it's my belief he never was in id at all at all, though the gintleman that tould me a heap more about it swears for sartin that he was." '

One of the earliest pictures to show people going under the Falls is the watercolour done in 1831 by Captain (later Sir) James Edward Alexander. In Alexander's picture a tiny figure can be seen hanging from the bridge built out from Goat Island at the brink of the Horseshoe Falls. This was Francis Abbott, the 'Hermit of Niagara', whose story fascinated Alexander and is told in his *Transatlantic Sketches.*

'From the end of the bridge there extended a single piece of timber, some twelve or fifteen feet over the cataract. On the bridge it was the daily practice of the hermit to walk, either when alone, or when there were visiters there, whom he often alarmed by his strange appearance in his dark gown, hair streaming in the wind, and bare feet. With a quick step he would pass along the bridge, advance on the timber to the extreme point, turn quickly but steadily on his heel, and walk back, and continue thus to walk to and fro for hours together. Sometimes he would stand on one leg, and pirouette with the other round the end of the log; then he would go down on his knees, and gaze in seeming ecstasy on the bright green and snow-white water of the cataract. "But the worst of all, Sir," said the ferryman to me, "was when he would let himself down by the hands, and hang over the Fall. Lord! Sir, my flesh used to creep, and my hair stand on end, when I saw him do that." '

Abbott had drowned a few weeks before Alexander visited the Falls. The strange solitary man had lived at Niagara for two years, and during much of that time had shunned all society and lived in isolation on Goat Island. 'When his cottage was examined hopes were entertained that some manuscript or memorial might be found of his composition; but he had left nothing of the kind ... A simple cot stood in one corner, and his guitar, violin, flute, and music-books, were scattered about confusedly; a portfolio lay on a rude table, and many leaves of a large book; but not a word, not even his name, was written on any of them.' The 'Hermit of Niagara' remained a romantic figure of mystery in every nineteenth-century guide-book.

The nonsense of the 'Maid of the Mist', the Indian maiden sent over the Falls as a sacrifice, did not become current until the turn of the century, although it first appeared many years earlier. The fictitious tale was published in *Burke's descriptive guide* of 1851, and Isabella Lucy Bird, who visited Niagara in 1854, quoted a guide's account of the story. It was, in fact, a gross distortion of a Seneca myth which tells how a maiden attempting suicide is saved by the god Hinu, who lives in a cave behind the Falls. She learns from him about the great snake who is responsible for the sickness and deaths in her village. When she returns there, she persuades the Indians to move away, but the serpent follows. Hinu kills the snake, which was so enormous that it became wedged in the rocks of the river. These gave way and thus formed the horseshoe shape that remains to this day.

In 1833 the Terrapin Tower was built on the brink of the Horseshoe Falls, on the rocks off Goat Island. Anna Jameson, who visited Niagara three years later, objected vehemently to 'the round tower, which some profane wretch has erected on the Crescent Fall; it stands there so detestably impudent and *mal-à-propos* – it is such a signal yet puny monument of bad taste – so miserably *mesquin*, and so presumptuous, that I do hope the violated majesty of nature will take the matter in hand, and overwhelm or cast it down the precipice one of these fine days, though indeed a barrel of gunpowder were a shorter if not a surer method'. Many years after the tower had been torn down as unsafe in 1873, W. D. Howells wrote in an essay of reminiscences of the Falls: 'There were many mysteries, maintained at a profit, about Niagara then, and not the least of them was Terrapin Tower ... The mystery of this was that any human being should wish to go up it at the risk of his life, but everybody did.' Not only did everybody visit it, but nearly every picture of the time included it, so that it became an integral part of the image of Niagara.

The tower could be seen in the famous painting by Frederick Edwin Church. When first exhibited in New York in 1857, Church's painting created a sensation. The *New York Daily News* declared it to be 'the great painting of the grandest subject of nature!' Seven and a half feet long and three and a half feet high, it showed the whole sweep of the Horseshoe Falls with such realism that it appeared to be 'a reflection thrown upon the canvas from a prism'. The *Boston Weekly Traveller* wrote that Church had rivalled Turner's light and equalled the detail of the Pre-Raphaelites – 'Not *as* the pre-Raphaelites, but with a conscientious finish of minuteness, which does not in the least clash with the broad beauty of the whole. The stones in the little round tower upon the American side of the Great Fall are perfectly made out, if you will look to see ...' Church's *tour de force*, now in the Corcoran Gallery, Washington, gains much from its considerable size and its impact is lost in reproduction. Fortunately this is not true of John Bornet's splendid lithograph, published two years earlier, which did not attract such attention then. It has not the realism of Church's painting, but captivates one today with its dramatic and romantic image.

A few early travellers remarked on the beauty of the Falls in winter, but it was not until the middle of the nineteenth century, and the advent of photography, that winter views became part of the image of Niagara. From the late 1850s onwards, photographs of the ice-covered landscape were part of the stock-in-trade of the souvenir stores. Only in the latter years of the century, however, were there many visitors to the Falls in winter; then the formation of an ice-bridge would attract hundreds of people.

'The name ice-bridge had deceived me,' wrote Howells, 'but the ice-bridge did not finally disappoint me. It is not a bridge at all. It is the channel of the river blocked as far as the eye can see down the gorge with huge squares and oblongs of ice, or of frozen snow, as they seem, and giving a realizing effect to all the remembered pictures of arctic scenery ... It was perfectly still that day, and in spite of the diapason of the Falls, an inner silence possessed the air. From the cliffs along the river the cedars thrust outward, armored in plates of ice, like the immemorial effigies of old-time warriors, and every cascade that had flung its bannerol of mist to the summer air, was now furled to the face of the rock and frozen fast. Again a sense of the repose, which is the secret of Niagara's charm, filled me.

'There was repose even in the peculiar traffic of Niagara when we penetrated to a shop devoted to the sale of its bric-à-brac for some photographs of the winter scenery, and we fancied a weird surprise and a certain statuesque reluctance in the dealer. But this may have been merely our fancy. I would insist only upon the mute immobility of the birds on the feather fans behind the glazed shelves, and a mystical remoteness in the Japanese objects mingled with the fabrics of our own Indians and the imported feldspar cups and vases.

'Our train went back to Buffalo through the early winter sunset, crimson and crimsoner over the rapids, and then purple over the ice where the river began to be frozen again. This color was so intense that the particles of ice along the brink were like a wilding growth of violets – those candied violets you see at the confectioner's.'

Mrs. Jameson stated that no writer had done justice to the beauty of the Falls. But it was not for want of trying. As Colonel Peter A. Porter, who was killed in the Civil War and whose family owned Goat Island and the American side of the Falls, wrote in a young lady's album nearly two centuries after Hennepin:

'What troops of tourists have encamped upon the river's brink;
What poets shed from countless quills, Niagaras of ink;
What artist armies tried to fix the evanescent bow
Of waters falling as they fell two hundred years ago.'

A

Hand-coloured engraving from the copy of
Hennepin's *Nouvelle decouverte*, 1697,
originally belonging to William III to whom the book is dedicated
Metropolitan Toronto Central Library

B

Cartouche from the map of North America by Herman Moll, 1715
Library of Congress

C

Columbia and Niagara
Mezzotint published shortly after the death of George Washington in 1799
Collection of J. Stuart Fleming

D

Watercolour by Thomas Davies, *c.* 1760
The New-York Historical Society

E

Watercolour by an unknown artist, *c.* 1828
Collection of J. Stuart Fleming
This watercolour was probably copied from a sketch
made some years earlier.

F

'Table Rock, Niagara'
Staffordshire transfer-printed plate by
E. Wood & Sons, *c.* 1835
This view of Table Rock was taken from
an engraving after a watercolour by
the Russian artist, Paul Svinin.
The engraving was one of the plates in Svinin's
Voyage pittoresque aux Etats-Unis de l'Amérique en 1811, 1812 et 1813,
first published in St. Petersburg in 1815.
The projecting shelf of rock on the
Canadian bank was sketched by many artists–
even after most of the rock
had fallen in 1850.

G

Etched and engraved label for a hair restorer, *c.* 1830
Library of Congress

H

'Niagara Falls, American Side'
by John Bornet
Coloured lithograph published by Goupil & Co.
New York, 1855

I

The Horseshoe Falls and Terrapin Tower
viewed from Goat Island
Painting by an unknown artist,
c. 1870

J

'Mighty Niagara': music cover, *c.* 1850,
with an engraving from Bartlett's *American Scenery*

K

View from below Table Rock
Watercolour by Sir James Edward Alexander, 1831
Royal Ontario Museum

L

Bank-note of the International Bank of Canada, 1858,
with an engraving from a daguerreotype of the
Terrapin Tower and Horseshoe Falls

M

The American Falls from Goat Island
Drawing by an unknown artist, *c.* 1840
This drawing has been copied from a lithograph of 1838,
which reproduces an earlier engraving
by W. J. Bennett, *c.* 1830.

N

Photograph by Alexander Henderson,
c. 1870

A

A View of ye Industry of ye Beavers of Canada in making Dams to stop ye Course of a Rivulet, in order to form a great Lake, about wch they build their Habitations. To Effect this; they fell large Trees with their Teeth, in such a manner as to make them come Cross ye Rivulet, to lay ye foundation of ye Dam; they make Mortar, work up, and finish ye whole with great order and wonderfull Dexterity.
The Beavers have two Doors to their Lodges, one to the Water and the other to the Land side. According to ye French Accounts.

B

To the
Memory of
GEO. WASHINGTON
Born 11th Feb. 1732.
Died 13th Dec.
1799.

C

D

E

F

OLDRIDGE'S
BALM OF COLUMBIA
FOR RESTORING HAIR
View of the Falls of Niagara
FOR RESTORING HAIR
No. 1 Wellington Street, Strand, London
Price 75 Cents
Sole Proprietor
London

G

H

I

MUSICAL BOUQUET.

MIGHTY NIAGARA,

A Descriptive Scena.

COMPOSED & SUNG WITH GREAT APPLAUSE BY

HENRY RUSSELL,

in his Popular Entertainment

"The Emigrant's Progress,"

THE POETRY BY CHARLES MACKAY, LL.D.

AND MOST RESPECTFULLY DEDICATED TO

Miss Sophia Davieson.

Henry Russell

LONDON: MUSICAL BOUQUET OFFICE, 192, HIGH HOLBORN; & J. ALLEN, 20, WARWICK LANE, PATERNOSTER ROW.

Nos 441 & 442. MUSICAL BOUQUET.

K

THE INTERNATIONAL BANK
OF CANADA
Will pay
on demand
One
Dollar
to the
Bearer
A
No. 15530
TORONTO,
CAPITAL $1,000,000.
For the International Bank
Danforth, Wright & Co. New York & Philada
CHARTERED BY ACT OF PARLIAMENT
FIVE SHILLINGS.
FIVE SHILLINGS.

L

M

N

FRONTIER

The Niagara River was within the territories of the 'Neutral' nation when the first Europeans arrived in the lower Great Lakes region. In 1651 the Neutrals were destroyed by the Iroquois and the river came under the control of that confederacy, who excluded the French and other Europeans from the region for more than ten years. However, the hold of the Iroquois eventually weakened, and by 1670 a number of French missionaries and traders had penetrated to Lake Ontario and beyond. La Salle's expedition of 1678 was the first serious attempt to establish French sovereignty over the Niagara region. On the east bank of the Niagara River, at its mouth, La Salle built a timber fort 'with two redoubts 40 feet square, upon a point easy of defense, made of great timbers, one upon another, musket-proof, and joined by a palisade', which he named Fort Conti. This fort, the first on or near the site of Fort Niagara, was destroyed by fire shortly after its erection in 1679 and was subsequently abandoned.

French sovereignty was disputed by the British. When Colonel Thomas Dongan, governor of the colony of New York, learned in 1686 that the French were proposing to re-establish the fort, he wrote to the Marquis de Denonville, governor of New France, that 'a place called Ohniagero on this side of the Lake [is] within my Masters territoryes without question'. Dongan licensed a trading expedition which crossed the Niagara portage on its way to the Upper Lakes, where the Indians gladly exchanged furs for rum instead of French brandy. Denonville was indignant: 'Think you, Sir, that Religion will make any progress whilst your merchants will supply, as they do, *eau de vie* in abundance, which as you ought to know, converts the savages into demons and their cabins into counterparts and theatres of hell.' Dongan agreed that the Indians should be 'dissuaded from their drunken debouches though certainly our Rum doth as little hurt as your Brandy and in the opinion of Christians is much more wholesome.' A second expedition from Albany in 1687 was captured by the French, who appropriated all the trading goods 'which by computation would have purchased to that Troop eight or nine thousand Beavers', after which 'the French divided all the Merchandize among the Indians, but kept the Rum to themselves, and got all drunk'.

Denonville built a second fort at Niagara, on nearly the same site as Fort Conti, in the summer of 1687 when he led a large force against the Senecas. His campaign was a failure. He only aroused the enmity of the Iroquois without destroying their power, and was forced to order the abandonment of the fort the next year, after a terrible winter during which practically the entire garrison died from scurvy, starvation, or Indian attacks.

In 1726 the French began the construction of Fort Niagara; it was completed the following year. William Burnet, governor of New York, protested unsuccessfully against the building of this large 'stone house', which with later alterations still stands today. At the same time, the Marquis de Beauharnois, governor of New France, demanded in vain that Burnet withdraw his garrison from the British fort, built in the spring of 1726, at the mouth of the Oswego on the southern shore of Lake Ontario, and 'cast down the block house and all pieces of work you raised up contrary to righteousness'.

The century-long struggle between the British and French for the domination of North America came to an end during the Seven Years' War. On July 25, 1759, nearly two months before Wolfe's capture of Quebec, Fort Niagara was surrendered after a short siege to Sir William Johnson, Superintendent of Indian Affairs, in command, at the time, of the attacking British forces. Captain Pouchot, who commanded the French garrison, described the surrender.

'On the 25th, between ten and eleven o'clock, the English sent four companies of grenadiers, four picquets, and a regiment into the fort. M. Pouchot drew up the garrison in line of battle upon the parade ground, their arms in their hands, and haversacks between their legs. He begged the officers to stay by their troops, and they remained in this situation about thirty hours. M. Pouchot had forewarned everybody of the necessity of this course, in order to protect themselves from the insults of the Indians ... He told them that if any Indian should come to strike them, or to take away anything, to give them a good kick in the bowels, or strike them with the fist in their stomachs, as the surest means of restraining them. If this would not check them, it would be better to die with arms in their hands, than be tortured by them. These orders were fulfilled exactly.

'The English had posted troops on every side to prevent the Indians from entering. They wished to induce the garrison to deliver their arms, under the pretext that they would then be in a better condition to defend us. M. Pouchot steadily refused this, and assured them that they could not then restrain the Indians from entering before we left. In fact, an hour after the English had entered the fort, the Indians scaled it on every side, and in half an hour after, there were more than five hundred in the fort. But they remained very quiet.

'The French officers had taken the precaution of putting a part of their equipages into the powder magazine. Every thing not thus secured was taken, either by the English officers or by detached soldiers. M. Pouchot gave a dinner to Colonel Johnson and some officers. After the dinner, these officers helped themselves to all the utensils and movables.'

The capitulation of New France took place at Montreal in 1760, but it was not until 1763 that the war ended in Europe with the Treaty of Paris, which ceded all of Canada to Great Britain. With the ending of hostilities, the fur trade was resumed and Fort Schlosser was built on the upper river at the end of the portage above the Falls, near the site of an earlier French fort built on the east bank at the beginning of the war.

In May 1763 the Indian uprising led by Pontiac broke out at Detroit. On September 14, several hundred Senecas ambushed a wagon train with a military escort on the Niagara portage near the whirlpool. Only two or three men escaped from the 'Devil's Hole Massacre'; one of them was John Stedman who had the contract for the operation of the portage. Two companies of the 80th Regiment, stationed at Fort Niagara, heard the firing and advanced on the run to investigate. These soldiers were caught in a second ambush and almost wiped out. The following year Sir William Johnson held an Indian council at Fort Niagara, at which the Senecas ceded a strip of land on both sides of the river as a partial reparation for these massacres. British control was strengthened the same year, 1764, by the building of Fort Erie on the west bank, at the inlet of the Niagara on Lake Erie.

Somewhat ironically, the extension of British rule in North America led almost directly to the American Revolution. During the revolution Fort Niagara became the headquarters of the Corps of Rangers commanded by Lieutenant-Colonel John Butler. The forays of Butler's Rangers and their Indian allies to Wyoming, Pennsylvania, and Cherry Valley, New York, in 1778 have been depicted in American popular history as the most fiendish of Loyalist atrocities, and Fort Niagara as a den of Tory infamy. 'There,' wrote Samuel De Veaux in his *Tourist's guide* of 1839, 'were congregated the leaders and chiefs of those bands of miscreants, that carried death and destruction into the remote American settlements. There, civilized Europe revelled with savage

America; and ladies of education and refinement mingled in the society of those whose only distinction was to wield the bloody tomahawk and scalping-knife. There, the squaws of the forest were raised to eminence, and the most unholy unions between them and officers of the highest rank, smiled upon and countenanced ... It was the depot of their plunders; there they planned their forays, and there they returned to feast, until the hour of action came again.'

The hardships and miseries of the Loyalist refugees, who found a haven at the fort, had no place in the American myth. In 1780 four or five Loyalist families settled on the west bank of the Niagara River. This side of the river was then wilderness with the exception of the recently established naval station at Navy Hall, nearly opposite to Fort Niagara, and Butler's Barracks which had been built to house the Rangers and their refugee families on the higher ground to the westward. More Loyalists cleared farms in the next two years, and their number greatly increased after the cessation of hostilities in 1783. These settlers, who by 1786 numbered nearly a thousand, were under the direct control of the government at Quebec until the creation of the Province of Upper Canada in 1791 (in 1841 Upper Canada became known as Canada West, and at confederation in 1867 it became the Province of Ontario). The first capital of the new province was the small village of Newark (now Niagara) which had been laid out two years earlier at the mouth of the river.

The east side of the Niagara River had become United States territory by the Treaty of Paris of 1783, but Fort Niagara remained in British hands until August 11, 1796, after the controversy over it and other northwestern forts, which were retained by the British in an attempt to enforce the full observance of the peace treaty, had been settled by Jay's Treaty of 1794. A new post, Fort George, was built on the west bank nearly a mile from Lake Ontario, and became the principal British fort on the Niagara frontier.

The frontier became a major battleground during the War of 1812. The causes of the war were ostensibly the British interference with United States trade with Napoleonic Europe, and the impressment of American seamen by the British navy. Congress, in its declaration of war on June 18, 1812, was, however, greatly influenced by the belief of the War Hawks that, as William Eustis, Secretary of War, stated, 'We can take Canada without soldiers! we have only to send officers into the Provinces, and the people, disaffected toward their own government, will rally to our standard'. The considerable American immigration that had followed the Loyalist settlement in Upper Canada suggested that there were good grounds for this belief. Major-General Isaac Brock, administrator of the province, wrote shortly after the outbreak of war: 'My situation is most critical, not from any thing the enemy can do, but from the disposition of the people – The population, believe me is essentially bad – A full belief possess them all that this Province must inevitably succumb ... Most of the people have lost all confidence – I however speak loud and look big.' Brock's brilliant capture of Detroit on August 16, and with it an American army that had attempted to invade Upper Canada, changed the picture. As Brock reported: 'The militia have been inspired, by the recent success, with confidence – the disaffected are silenced.'

The second attempted invasion of the province took place across the Niagara River at Queenston. Major-General Stephen Van Rensselaer, with a force of more than four thousand men, launched the expected attack on October 13, 1812. Brock hastened from Fort George to the scene of action, and was killed while leading a counter-attack against the Americans who had captured a gun on the heights above the village. Major-General Roger Hale Sheaffe assumed the British command. He left two six-pounders of the Royal Artillery, together with a detachment of infantry, to hold the village and prevent the passage of American reinforcements across the river. Then, with the remainder of his regular and militia forces, he climbed the escarpment by a path in the rear of some woods occupied by a party of Indians that were harassing the American troops led by Lieutenant-Colonel Winfield Scott. The news of the Indian attacks created a panic among the state militia that were waiting to be ferried over, and Van Rensselaer 'found that ... the ardor of the unengaged troops had entirely subsided'; they refused to cross the river. When Sheaffe ordered a general advance, the American position on the heights was carried almost without resistance, and the American troops were forced back upon the river, where they discovered they had been abandoned by their boats. Nearly one thousand men, including Winfield Scott, surrendered; the British losses were fourteen killed, seventy-seven wounded, and twenty-one missing. Sheaffe was created a baronet for his victory at Queenston Heights, but it was Sir Isaac Brock – the news of his knighthood awarded for his success at Detroit did not reach Canada until after his death – who became 'the hero of Upper Canada'.

Van Rensselaer relinquished his command and was replaced by Brigadier-General Alexander Smyth, whose brief campaign on the upper river was a curious fiasco. Several thousand regulars and militia were encamped at Buffalo, but these troops were mainly raw recruits, poorly officered and equipped. 'They appear to be almost as ignorant of their duty as if they had never seen a camp, and scarcely know on which shoulder to carry the musket,' an inspecting officer reported of a regular regiment. 'They are mere militia, and if possible even worse, and if taken into action in their present state will prove more dangerous to themselves than to their enemy.'

On November 10, 1812, Smyth issued a proclamation 'to the men of the State of New York', described by the American historian, Henry Adams, as 'written in a style hitherto unusual in American warfare'. Smyth followed it a week later with another addressed to his troops. 'The time is at hand,' he declared, 'when you will cross the streams of Niagara, to conquer Canada, and to secure the peace of the American frontier.' On November 27, he issued a general order for the embarkation of his forces: 'Friends of your Country! Ye who have "the will to do, the heart to dare", the moment you have wished for has arrived. Think on your country's honor lost, her rights trampled, her sons enslaved, her infants perishing by the hatchet. Be strong! be brave! and let the ruffian power of the English King cease on this continent.' In the early hours of November 28, two assault parties crossed the river, but were eventually driven back by British troops from Fort Erie. A council of war then decided to postpone the invasion by a large body of Smyth's forces, who 'were ordered to disembark and dine'. However, the next day a manifesto announced: 'Hearts of War! Tomorrow will be memorable in the annals of the United States.' On the morning of November 30, more than a thousand troops entered the waiting boats, but again a council of war decided to halt the expedition and the soldiers were ordered to disembark. Peter Buell Porter, who had been one of the leading War Hawks and had resigned his congressional seat at the beginning of the war to become a brigadier-general in the New York state militia, accused Smyth of being a coward. The two men fought a harmless duel on Grand Island; after an exchange of shots, they shook hands and dined together the same evening. In December 1812 Smyth was granted leave to visit his family in Virginia; he never returned to duty.

As the war developed, action took place on both land and water in many widely separated parts of North America, but the Niagara frontier continued to be a major line of attack by American forces. In this, American plans were much more influenced by political and practical considerations than by strategical theory. The war was popular in the western sections of New York and Pennsylvania, and the newly organized territories west of the Appalachians; here supplies were easily raised and valuable bodies of militia were recruited, as, for example, the mounted riflemen from Kentucky. Along the frontier east of Oswego to the Atlantic, most of the people were either indifferent or definitely opposed to the war, and they refused to take any measures in support of the military or even to desist from trading with Canada. Furthermore, it was in the southern peninsula of Upper Canada that there seemed to be the best opportunity of seizing territory with a good soil and climate, particularly since the defences of British North America were based upon the Royal Navy and the fortress of Quebec, hundreds of miles away to the east and only reached by long and difficult lines of communication.

The years 1813 and 1814 witnessed a see-saw battle on the Niagara frontier.

A large American force captured Fort George in May 1813. Fort Erie was evacuated and the British troops on the frontier retreated westwards. On the night of June 5, two American brigadier-generals were captured in a surprise attack on their encampment at Stoney Creek, and the next day the American force retired towards Niagara. A second American disaster took place less than three weeks later, when nearly six hundred cavalry and infantry, together with two field guns, surrendered after being ambushed by a smaller Indian force at Beaver Dams. Fort George remained in American hands, however, until December 10, when Brigadier-General George McClure ordered its evacuation. Before the American soldiers retired across the river, the village of Newark was set on fire and destroyed on McClure's orders. Nine days later, a force of more than five hundred British regulars stormed Fort Niagara, which was then retained in British hands until the end of the war. The American frontier was devastated by British troops in retaliation for the burning of Newark, which had left several hundred women and children homeless in the middle of winter. Youngstown, Lewiston, Manchester (Niagara Falls), Schlosser, and Buffalo were destroyed.

The fiercest fighting of the war took place in 1814. On July 3, two American brigades crossed the river above the Falls; the next morning the brigade commanded by Winfield Scott, who had been released in an exchange of prisoners, advanced along the road to Chippawa, where an engagement took place on July 5. The efficiency of the American musketry and artillery fire forced the retreat of the British troops commanded by Major-General Phineas Riall. Scott's brigade wore grey uniforms in this battle, and in commemoration of their success, grey was adopted as the colour of the uniform for the cadets at the United States Military Academy at West Point. The most hard fought battle of the entire war took place on July 25 at Lundy's Lane, almost within sight of the Falls. Attack and counter-attack continued until midnight, when the Americans under Major-General Jacob Brown withdrew leaving the exhausted British soldiers commanded by Lieutenant-General Gordon Drummond in possession of the field. Riall was wounded and taken prisoner; Drummond, Brown, and Scott were severely wounded. Fort Erie, which had been captured by American forces on the first day of the campaign, was retained as a bridgehead, in spite of a fierce British assault, until November when the garrison was withdrawn to Buffalo.

A British offer to negotiate a peace settlement had been accepted by President Madison in January 1814, but it was not until August that negotiations began at Ghent. Before the news of the signing of the peace treaty on Christmas Eve had reached America, Major-General Andrew Jackson had won an impressive victory on January 8, 1815, against an invading British army at

New Orleans. There were more than two thousand British casualties, while American losses totalled seventy-one killed and wounded. Jackson's victory ended the war in a blaze of glory that convinced Americans that they had won it. The unexpectedly successful defence of Canada, on the other hand, led to a Canadian tradition of a victory against overwhelming odds.

Neither blockade nor impressment were mentioned in the Treaty of Ghent, which was based on a return to the *status quo* before the war. It did, however, establish that the boundary between the United States and British North America was to be defined by a number of commissions. A survey was made in 1819 that established the boundary line 'through the middle of Lake Ontario until it strikes the communication between that lake and Lake Erie, thence along the middle of said communication into Lake Erie'. The American survey party camped on Goat Island. Major Joseph Delafield, one of the surveyors, wrote in his diary: 'The noise of the rapids and falls ... is rather a lullaby than an antidote to sleep. The whole island appears to tremble under my pillow, yet I as well as the whole party rested perfectly throughout the night.'

The continuous peace that has been maintained between Canada and the United States since the War of 1812 has tended to obscure the latent hostility which existed for many years between the two countries. During the Mackenzie rebellion it seemed for a while as though war would break out again on the Niagara frontier. William Lyon Mackenzie, editor of the *Colonial advocate*, who had been one of the leaders of a reform movement in Upper Canada, had been defeated in the provincial election of 1836, when Sir Francis Bond Head, the lieutenant-governor, assumed the leadership of the conservatives and successfully branded the reformers as being disloyal to the British connection. When a rebellion in the province of Lower Canada drew off the regular forces from Upper Canada, Mackenzie called for a similar insurrection, but his erratic and unstable extremism had already antagonized the majority of reformers and the uprising was a fiasco. Seven to eight hundred rebels gathered at Montgomery's Tavern, about two miles north of Toronto, on the night of December 4, 1837. The next day their advance-guard was fired on by a small picket of volunteers from the city. After firing their muskets the volunteers took to their heels, but so did the rebels, who were completely routed by a larger militia force the following day. Mackenzie fled around the head of Lake Ontario to the Niagara frontier, and escaped across the river to Grand Island.

When Mackenzie arrived at Buffalo on December 11, he received an enthusiastic welcome. At a public meeting the next evening, he gave a dramatic review of the struggle against British 'tyranny' in America, and then asked for arms, ammunition, and volunteers. Many enlisted 'for the commendable purpose of aiding and assisting our Canadian brethren in their present struggle for liberty', and Rensselaer Van Rensselaer, grandson of the general commanding at Queenston Heights and 'a young man of more ambition than brains', was appointed 'general' in command. Two days later Mackenzie and Van Rensselaer established their headquarters on Navy Island, on the Canadian side of the Niagara River two miles above the Falls. There Mackenzie as 'Chairman pro tem. of the Provisional Government of the State of Upper Canada' issued a proclamation outlining his aims and promising 'three hundred acres of the best of the publick lands' to every volunteer who joined the Patriot standard.

In order to avoid an imbroglio with the United States, no direct action was taken at first to oust the rebels. However, Colonel Allan MacNab, commanding the militia encamped along the Canadian shore near Chippawa, presently learned that the American steamer *Caroline* was ferrying men and supplies to the Patriots, and suggested to Captain Andrew Drew that the ship be destroyed. On the night of December 29, Drew, a half-pay naval officer serving with the Canadian militia, set out with a party of volunteers in small boats. They found the *Caroline* tied up at the wharf at Fort Schlosser, boarded her, and after a brief struggle forced the crew and about twenty men, who were sleeping on board, ashore. The ship was then cut away, set on fire, and sent down the river in flames. She broke up in the rapids, but parts of her went over the Falls, and her figurehead was salvaged near Lewiston. Two weeks later Mackenzie and his 'Patriot Army' withdrew from Navy Island.

Wildly exaggerated reports of Drew's action caused an uproar in the United States. Governor William L. Marcy of New York stated that 'probably more than one-third' of the thirty-three persons on board were 'wantonly massacred', when in fact only one man had been killed in the skirmish. Popular indignation was so great that war seemed imminent, but President Van Buren was determined to preserve the peace. General Winfield Scott was sent to the frontier to assume command of the state militia and prevent any further incidents. At the same time the United States Government demanded redress from Great Britain for the violation of American territory. The matter was finally settled during the discussions between Daniel Webster and Lord Ashburton prior to the Treaty of Washington of 1842, when Ashburton assured Webster that 'no slight or disrespect to the sovereign authority of the Unites States' had been intended, and that he regretted 'that some explanation and apology for this occurrence was not immediately made'.

The *Caroline* incident, however, had encouraged American sympathizers to join the Patriot cause and engage in filibustering, and the efforts of Winfield Scott and other federal officials were not sufficient to prevent a series of raids over the Canadian border in 1838 and 1839. Pillaging by freebooters, on the other hand, did not persuade responsible American opinion of 'the propriety of a war between the United States and Great Britain for the purpose of "liberating" the Canadians from the state which a very great majority are perfectly contented with'. In 1839 both Mackenzie and Van Rensselaer were convicted of having violated the neutrality laws and were imprisoned. The Patriot movement eventually petered out with such futile provocations as the abortive attempt in 1840 to blow up Brock's monument at Queenston Heights. The damaged Tuscan pillar, which had been erected in 1824, was eventually replaced in 1853-56 by the present monument – a florid triumphal column surmounted by a colossal statue of the general – 'erected chiefly by the voluntary contributions of the militia and Indian warriors' of the province.

During the troubled period, the Canadian militia were reinforced by British regulars. The parades of the 43rd Regiment, which encamped by the Horseshoe Falls in 1839, became a great attraction to American tourists. Lieutenant (later Sir) Richard G. A. Levinge portrayed the enjoyable side of soldiering on the Niagara frontier in winter in his print of the regimental officers in their sleighs. Its other aspects were described in his *Echoes from the backwoods*: 'It was the duty of the orderly-officer to visit every night a guard placed at the ferry below the Falls, at a short distance from them. A narrow path led down to where this guard was stationed, and it was anything but agreeable, on a dark night, to find one's way down a frozen, slippery path, beset with monster icicles, which, hanging overhead, threatened destruction at every step ... When on these guards several sentinels were fired at. Little urchins, from the other side of the river, would shy an axe into a tree, and, making a rest of it, take a deliberate shot at them.'

Relations between the United States and the British North American provinces were strained during the Civil War by incidents such as the *Trent* affair, and the St. Albans raid. After the war there was, as a result, a considerable American sympathy for the Fenian Brotherhood, which planned to win Ireland's independence by a ludicrous scheme to invade and conquer Canada as a means of exerting pressure on Great Britain. On May 31, 1866, 'General' John O'Neill crossed the Niagara River from Black Rock with about eight hundred men. A skirmish took place on June 2 at Ridgeway, seven miles west of Fort Erie, between the Fenians, who had been reinforced and now totalled about twelve hundred, and a smaller force of Canadian militia, which had been hastily mobilized and rushed to the frontier. The Canadians withdrew in considerable confusion after suffering some casualties. The Fenians, however, gained nothing from their advantage, and before a column of British regulars had arrived, O'Neill prudently retreated across the river, where he and many of his followers were arrested by the commander of the United States gunboat *Michigan*.

The discomfiture of the virtually untrained militia at Ridgeway was the subject of a humorous Canadian pamphlet, written under the pseudonym of Doscen Gauust: 'Fortune at last decided what valor was unable to achieve, Major Gilmour, who now for the first time was seen by any of his men, by some inexplicable concatenation of circumstances allowed himself to be carried into the very thickest of the fight. Being mounted he of course attracted the notice of the enemy and immediately became the mark for a hundred sharpshooters. Before he could extricate himself from a position the last in the world he either expected or intended to occupy, a Fenian bullet pierced his fieldglass and he fell to the earth exclaiming, "I'm killed – my glass, oh, my glass!" The fall of their follower naturally caused the greatest consternation among the troops. Firing was at once suspended, swords reeking with sweat and dust returned to their scabbards, smelling bottles thrust at the nose of the fallen hero and messengers at once dispatched for surgeons to attend to the wounded field-glass. It was during this lull and frenzied excitement that the Fenian leader ordered the final charge. They came on with a true Milesian yell, and before the men of the Queen's Own could recover from the shock caused by the lamentable accident which had deprived them of their commanding officer, the color-sergeant was overpowered, the standard secured, and the enemy retiring in triumph. The victory was dearly purchased, not less than seventy-five thousand mosquitoes being left dead on the field from suffocation by smoke and fright at the unearthly yells of the savage combatants.'

O'Neill's raid was the last incursion on the Niagara frontier. The few later Fenian raids, elsewhere, were dismal failures, but United States animosity encouraged the British North American provinces to take the Fenian threat seriously, and the 'American menace' was a major factor in the movement that led to Canadian confederation in 1867.

A

Map by Michael De Bruls, *c.* 1759
Buffalo & Erie County Historical Society

B

Fort Niagara
Watercolour by an unknown artist, late 18th century
Royal Ontario Museum

C

'The Esplanade, Fort-George, Upper Canada'
Watercolour by Edward Walsh, 1805
Clements Library

D

'Old Fort-Erie, with the Migrations of the Wild Pidgeon in Spring'
Watercolour by Edward Walsh, 1804
Royal Ontario Museum
Lieutenant Edward Walsh
was a surgeon with the 49th Regiment of Foot.
The withdrawal of the regiment to Europe
after ten years service in Canada
was cancelled on the outbreak of war in 1812.
Brock led two companies of the 49th Regiment,
together with men of the Lincoln militia,
in the ill-fated charge
at the battle of Queenston Heights
in which he was killed.

E

Battle of Queenston Heights
13 October 1812
Coloured engraving, drawn by Major Dennis
and engraved by T. Sutherland, 1836
Royal Ontario Museum

F

First proclamation of
Brigadier-General Alexander Smyth
10 November 1812
Buffalo & Erie County Historical Society

G

'SOLDIERS on a march to BUFFALO'
Cartoon by William Charles, 1813
The New-York Historical Society

H

Major-General Sir Isaac Brock
From a pastel by William Berczy, 1811
Public Archives of Canada

I

Major-General Winfield Scott
From an engraving in the *Analectic Magazine*
December 1814
Library of Congress

J

Brigadier-General Peter B. Porter
From a miniature by Anson Dickinson, 1817
Buffalo & Erie County Historical Society

K

Medal by Thomas Wyon Jr
for the Loyal and Patriotic Society of Upper Canada, 1813
Royal Ontario Museum
The Society could not agree on how the medals were to be awarded,
and in 1840 all but three were defaced and sold as bullion.
In later years restrikes have been made
from the original dies.

L

'Fort Erie [American] Defence of the Block House'
Coloured lithograph by A. N. Childs
from a drawing by E. W. Clay
probably *c.* 1830
Royal Ontario Museum

M

'The CAROLINE Steam Boat Precipitated over the Falls of Niagara'
Coloured engraving, *c.* 1838
Collection of J. Stuart Fleming

N

Figurehead of the *Caroline*
Buffalo & Erie County Historical Society

O

Patriot handbill, 1837
Buffalo & Erie County Historical Society

P

'The "43rd Light Infantry" as they "turn out" in their sleighs;
at the "Falls of Niagara", 1839'
Coloured engraving from
a drawing by Sir Richard Levinge
Metropolitan Toronto Central Library

Q

Cartoon by Thomas Nast
Niagara Mohawk Power Corporation

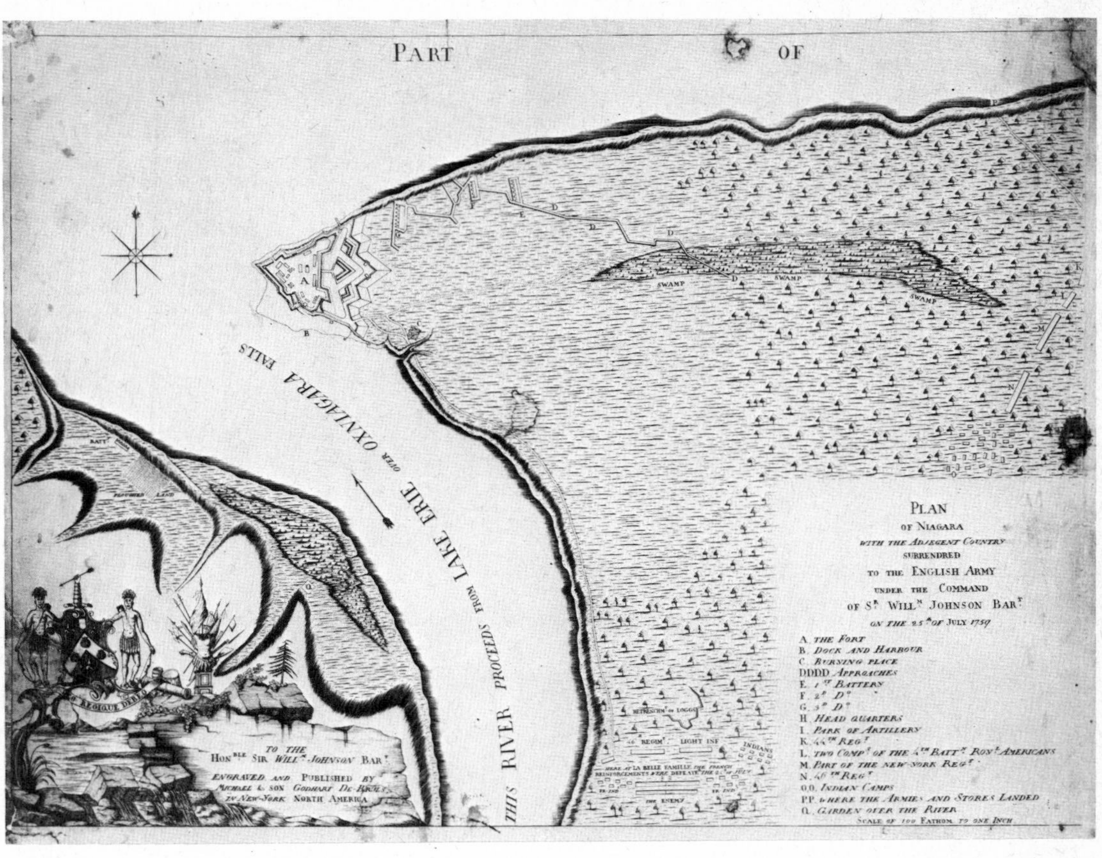
PART OF
SWAMP
SWAMP
SWAMP
THIS RIVER PROCEEDS FROM LAKE ERIE OVER OXNIAGARA FALLS
PLAN
OF NIAGARA
WITH THE ADJEGENT COUNTRY
SURRENDRED
TO THE ENGLISH ARMY
UNDER THE COMMAND
OF SR. WILLM. JOHNSON BART.
ON THE 25TH OF JULY 1759
A. THE FORT
B. DOCK AND HARBOUR
C. BURNING PLACE
DDDD APPROACHES
E. 1ST BATTERY
F. 2D. DO.
G. 3D. DO.
H. HEAD QUARTERS
I. PARK OF ARTILLERY
K. 44TH REGT.
L. TWO COMPS. OF THE 4TH BATTN. ROYL. AMERICANS
M. PART OF THE NEW-YORK REGT.
N. 46TH REGT.
O.O. INDIAN CAMPS
P.P. WHERE THE ARMIES AND STORES LANDED
Q. GARDEN OVER THE RIVER
SCALE OF 100 FATHOM TO ONE INCH
TO THE
HONBLE. SIR WILLM. JOHNSON BART.
ENGRAVED AND PUBLISHED BY
MICHAEL & SON GODHART DE-BRULS
IN NEW-YORK NORTH AMERICA

A

B

C

Old Fort-Erie; with the Migrations of the Wild-Pidgeon in Spring taken April 18th 1804

D

THE BATTLE OF QUEENSTON, OCT.R 13TH 1812.
Which ended in a complete Victory on the part of the British, having captured 927 Men, killed or wounded about 500.
Taken 1400 Stand of Arms, a six Pounder, and a Stand of Colours.

E

BUFFALO GAZETTE...EXTRA.

TO THE MEN OF THE STATE OF NEW YORK.

FOR many years you have seen your country oppressed with numerous wrongs. Your Government, although above all others devoted to Peace, have been forced to draw the Sword, and rely for redress of injuries on the valor of the American People.

That valor has been conspicuous. But the nation has been unfortunate in the selection of some of those who have directed it. One Army has been disgracefully surrendered and lost. Another has been sacrificed by a precipitate attempt to pass it over at the strongest point of the enemy's lines, with most incompetent means. The cause of these miscarriages is apparent. The commanders were popular men, "destitute alike of theory and experience" in the art of war.

In a few days, the troops under my command will plant the American Standard in Canada. They are men accustomed to obedience, silence, and steadiness. They will conquer, or they will die.

Will you stand with your arms folded, and look on this interesting struggle? Are you not related to the men who fought at Bennington and Saratoga? Has the race degenerated? Or have you under the baleful influence of contending factions forgot your Country? Must I turn from you, and ask the men of the *Six Nations* to support the Government of the United States? Shall I imitate the officers of the British King, and suffer our ungathered laurels to be tarnished by ruthless deeds? Shame, where is thy blush? No. Where I command, the vanquished and the peaceful man, the child, the maid, and the matron, shall be secure from wrong. If we conquer, we will "conquer but to save."

MEN OF NEW YORK!

The present is the hour of renown. Have you not a wish for fame? Would you not choose in future times to be named as one of those, who, imitating the heroes whom Montgomery led, have in spite of the seasons, visited the tomb of the chief, and conquered the country where he lies? Yes. You desire your share of fame. Then seize the present moment. If you do not, you will regret it; and say, "The valiant have bled in vain: The friends of my country fell—and I was not "there."

Advance then to our aid. I will wait for you a few days. I cannot give you the day of my departure. But come on. Come in companies, half companies, pairs, or singly. I will organize you for a short tour. Ride to this place, if the distance is far, and send back your horses. But remember, that every man who accompanies us, places himself under my command; and shall submit to the salutary restraints of discipline.

ALEXANDER SMYTH,
BRIGADIER GENERAL.

Camp near Buffalo,
10th Nov. 1812.

SOLDIERS *on a march to* BUFFALO.

G

H

I

J

K

FORT ERIE. DEFENCE OF THE BLOCK HOUSE.

The CAROLINE Steam Boat Precipitated over the Falls of Niagara Dec. 29 1837

M

N

PATRIOT

VOLUNTEERS,

Will Rensdezvous THIS EVENING, at 9 o'clock, in front of the THEATRE, prepared to take up the line of march.

By order of the Commanding Officer.

***Buffalo, Dec.* 13, 1837.**

THE "43RD" LIGHT INFANTRY, AS THEY "TURN OUT" IN THEIR SLEIGHS, AT THE "FALLS OF NIAGARA." 1839.

"SHOOTING NIAGARA."
The invasion of Great Britain by the way of Canada.

EXPANSION

The Niagara frontier quickly recovered from the destruction that had taken place during the War of 1812. In 1816 James Monroe succeeded James Madison as president of the United States; Monroe's administration became known as 'The Era of Good Feelings', because of the lessening of internal political animosities that took place with a surge of national pride following the war. It was an era not only of 'good feelings' in the United States, but also of unprecedented growth and expansion on both sides of the border. Frances Wright, an English traveller, wrote in 1818 that though 'some faint traces of the war' could still be seen, 'the villages and towns have indeed sprung up like the Phenix from her ashes'.

Water was supreme as a means of communication in the newly settled and developing countries, and shipping on Lakes Ontario and Erie grew with the demands of merchants, immigrants, and settlers. Paddle steamers began to appear on the lakes. On September 7, 1816, the first steamboat on Lake Ontario, the *Frontenac*, was launched at Finkle's Point on the Bay of Quinte. The first American steamer was the *Ontario*, which began running between Ogdensburgh and Lewiston in 1817, and the following year the *Walk-in-the-Water*, launched at Black Rock, became the first steamboat to ply on Lake Erie. In his *Sketches of Upper Canada* published only three years later, in 1821, John Howison remarked with some exaggeration that 'the steam-boat now monopolizes almost all the carrying business'. The Niagara River linked the two lakes, but the Falls and rapids had to be by-passed by a slow and expensive portage.

John Stedman's contract for the original portage on the east side of the river had been due to expire in 1791, but in 1790, before the east bank had been relinquished to the United States, Lord Dorchester, the governor-general, ordered that a Canadian portage road be officially established on the west side of the river from Queenston to Chippawa. The portage was re-opened on the American side by Porter, Barton & Company under a lease from the State of New York in 1805. This firm, in which Augustus Porter and Peter B. Porter were two of the partners, owned or controlled ships on both lakes, and had warehouses at Lewiston, Schlosser and Black Rock. Freight from New York was loaded onto their vessels at Oswego, on Lake Ontario, and carried to the head of navigation on the lower river at Lewiston, opposite Queenston. From there ox-teams carried it seven miles over the portage to Fort Schlosser, where it was transferred to the firm's Durham boats which were poled up-river to Black Rock. From Black Rock freight was carried by their ships on Lake Erie to Cleveland and Detroit, or transferred to boats passing through Lake Chatauqua into the Alleghany River to Pittsburgh. This highly profitable business came to an end in 1825, with the completion of the state-built Erie Canal from Albany on the Hudson River to Buffalo on Lake Erie.

A canal on the Canadian side of the Niagara River was first suggested in 1818 by William Hamilton Merritt, a merchant at St. Catharine's. The *Montreal Gazette* (23 September 1818) welcomed his proposal: 'The two greatest and almost the only obstructions in the navigation from the Lakes to Montreal, are the La Chine and Niagara carrying places, were these removed by means of Canals, the trade of the settlements on each side of the Lakes and River would glide into this port, nor would there be any reason to fear that the great American Canal now making could divert it to New-York.' In fact, the Erie Canal was to do just that, and the American and much of the Canadian western trade, which had come over the Niagara portage and down the St. Lawrence, now took the easier and cheaper route by the new canal to New York.

Merritt's Welland Canal Company was incorporated in 1824, and late in 1829 two schooners passed through the canal that extended from the site of Port Dalhousie on Lake Ontario to the Welland River, which flowed into the Niagara at Chippawa. An extension of this canal, completed in 1833, carried it through to Port Colborne on Lake Erie, thus avoiding the difficult navigation of the Niagara River.

The *Buffalo Republican Extra*, which reported the arrival of the two schooners, suggested that the event might 'give an impetus to our national or state governments, or a body corporate, in making a canal or rail-way, from the Niagara river at Schlosser, to the same river, at Lewiston'. This was not a new suggestion, for as early as 1798 the State of New York had passed an act incorporating 'the Niagara company, for the purpose of making a canal, with locks, around the Niagara Falls'. No work was done on this project, and at the end of ten years the company's charter lapsed. There were many other proposals for such a canal, and President Jackson commissioned an official survey in 1835 by the topographical engineers of the United States Army. In March of the following year, Captain W. G. Williams submitted his report on the survey, which, if it did nothing else, inspired one of the most gloriously fanciful prints relating to Niagara.

Any commercial practicality for an American ship canal around the Falls had been destroyed by the 363-mile Erie Canal, which was to play a major role in establishing the prosperity of New York State and ensuring the primacy of the port of New York. The Erie was an immediate financial success, and by 1878, five years before its tolls were abolished, had paid into the state treasury forty-two million dollars more than its cost of construction, enlargement, and operation. The Welland Canal, on the other hand, did not attract the expected American trade and was to remain heavily in debt. Its financial difficulties were made worse by cheap construction that led to continual and expensive repairs, and the Welland Canal Company had eventually to be bought out by the Province of Canada. However, the dashing of the over-optimistic hopes for the Canadian waterway did not deter the promoters of Canadian railways from having similarly unrealistic expectations.

The first railways at Niagara were built to attract packet passengers on the Erie Canal to the Falls. In July 1836 the *Niagara Falls Journal* reported that the Lockport & Niagara Falls Railroad was rapidly approaching completion, and that cars were running on parts of the Buffalo & Niagara Falls Railroad. Both railways used horse-drawn cars at first, but an advertisement dated August 23, 1837, in the *Niagara Democrat* announced: 'Two trips per day, by steam power, are now performed to and from Lower Lockport and Niagara Falls ... The trips are performed in about an hour and 40 minutes, including stops, distance 24 miles ... By the Buffalo and Niagara Falls railroad, passengers are taken from the Falls to Buffalo in less than two hours; distance 23 miles.' The track of the two roads was similar; long iron straps were spiked to the wooden rails, and the ties rested on planks laid lengthwise.

'Those old rails made us a good deal of trouble', Stephen Sult, who had been construction foreman on the Lockport & Niagara Falls Railroad, was quoted as saying in an interview published by the *Lockport Union* in 1893. 'They [the iron straps] were forever getting loose at the ends and running up over the car wheels.

'I remember seeing a passenger considerable surprised once by having the end of a rail come up through the floor of the car and knock off his hat. The engine used to run out of fuel sometimes, but that wasn't anything. All the fireman had to do was to stop and take a few rails from a farm fence.

'One time, though, we dumped out the President of the United States. It was sometime along in '37 or '38 that Martin Van Buren came up on the packet on his way to Niagara Falls, taking the train at Lockport. About a mile this side of Suspension Bridge a spread rail ditched the train, and the car the President sat in tumbled over on its side and the passengers were pitched together in a heap. The train was going so slow that nobody was hurt. The President crawled out without a scratch, and didn't look as if he was mad any. He helped tip the car back, climbed in, and on they went just as if nothing had happened.'

In 1843 canal and steamboat interests protested in vain to the New York state legislature against the 'effort ... now making on the part of the different rail-road companies between the Hudson river and Lake Erie, to form a combination and union of interests, in such manner as to create one great powerful monopoly out of many small monopolies'. Ten years later, the string of short lines which partially followed the route of the Erie Canal, and operated trains that were advertised as running from Buffalo 'Through to Albany in 25 Hours!', were consolidated into the New York Central Railroad.

The first railway in Upper Canada, the Erie & Ontario, ran from the steamboat landing at Queenston, past the Falls 'where you obtain[ed] just a glimpse and no more of the Cataract', to the harbour at Chippawa. It too was a 'strap' railway, and used horses exclusively from 1839 when it began operating until 1854 when it was rebuilt and extended northward to the town of Niagara. Like the Lockport & Niagara Falls Railroad, the Erie & Ontario did not operate in winter; it did not pay to clear the tracks of snow, when navigation had ceased and there were few travellers to the Falls.

William Hamilton Merritt, who had been responsible for the building of the Welland Canal, was also responsible for the establishment of the Niagara Falls International Bridge Company which was incorporated by the State of New York in 1846, and the Niagara Falls Suspension Bridge Company which was incorporated by the Province of Canada in the same year. The associated bridge companies requested a number of leading engineers to submit their opinions on a proposed combined road and railway bridge to be built about two miles below the Falls. This was not the first attempt to bridge the Niagara River. Ten years earlier a company was formed to build a bridge at Queenston–Lewiston. This company operated a small bank at Queenston for four years, but nothing came of its plan to erect a chain suspension bridge.

The depth of the Niagara River and its furious current, to say nothing of the enormous ice jams in winter, made it quite impossible to construct piers or falsework. The only structure that could be built at the time with a span long enough to bridge the 700-foot gorge without intermediate supports was a suspension bridge, and the practicability of a railway suspension bridge was doubtful. Only Charles Ellet, John A. Roebling, and two other engineers considered the project feasible.

In November 1847 the contract for the construction of the bridge was awarded to Ellet, an American-born engineer who had studied briefly at the École Polytechnique in Paris and had pioneered in the building of wire-cable suspension bridges. In 1846 he had begun the building of the first long-span, wire-cable, suspension bridge in the world, at Wheeling over the Ohio River. This bridge, which had a main span of 1,010 feet, was almost completely destroyed by a storm in 1854, five years after it was opened, and was afterwards reconstructed by Roebling.

In the spring of 1848 Ellet began the building of a temporary span at Niagara, to be used as a service bridge during the construction of the permanent bridge. As a means of getting men and supplies across the river, Ellet first built a basket ferry – a light iron car, fitted with two wooden seats, which ran on a wire cable suspended between two wooden towers on opposite banks of the gorge. The basket ferry was used by the public, as well as by the construction workers, until the temporary wooden suspension bridge was completed in July 1848. The tolls levied for the public use of the basket ferry and the suspension bridge became the subject of a dispute between Ellet and the directors of the bridge companies, as a result of which Ellet resigned at the end of the year.

No immediate action was taken to progress further with the planned railway bridge, since no railway, except the little horse-operated Erie & Ontario, was running on the Canadian side of the river. However, in 1851 the construction of the Great Western Railway finally began after more than fifteen years of talk. There was considerable American interest and investment in this railway, which was to be a trunk line running from the Niagara River, via Hamilton, to Windsor, thereby connecting the lines that were shortly to be consolidated into the New York Central with the Michigan Central at Detroit. A railway bridge across the Niagara had now become a necessity; the contract for it was offered this time to John Augustus Roebling.

Roebling, who was born in Mühlhausen, Thuringia, in 1806, had graduated as a civil engineer from the Royal Polytechnic School, Berlin, in 1826. Five years later, his liberal republican views forced him to emigrate to the United States, where he became one of the greatest engineers of the nineteenth century. His Niagara Suspension Bridge was to be the first successful railway suspension bridge in the world; its span of 821 feet was nearly double that of any previous railway bridge. Roebling's last and greatest design was the Brooklyn Bridge, which he never lived to see. His right foot was crushed in an accident during the final survey for this bridge, and he died from tetanus on July 22, 1869, before construction began.

Roebling's original plan for the Niagara bridge had been for a single-deck structure with a railway track in the centre, but he now changed his design to a double-deck bridge with a 'carriage and footway' eighteen feet below the railway deck. The longest railway span in the world at the time was Robert Stephenson's Britannia Bridge across the Menai Straits. This iron tubular bridge was supported on three massive stone piers, and four huge sculptured lions were placed at the imposing approaches to it. Roebling probably had Stephenson's great bridge in mind when he wrote to the directors of the bridge companies in July 1852: 'The appearance of the double-floor bridge will not be so beautiful as will a single floor, with imposing gateways, erected in the massive Egyptian style, and joined by massive wings; the cables watched by sphinxes, with parapets and all the rest of the approaches put up of appropriate dimensions, and in suitable style. The double-floor bridge ... will, however, present a very graceful, simple, but, at the same time, substantial appearance. The four massive cables, supported on isolated columns, of a very substantial make, will form the characteristic of the work; and this will be unique and striking in its effect and quite in keeping with the surrounding scenery.'

The four ten-inch cables rested on heavy limestone pillars with a distinct taper and 'Egyptian' capitals. These cables carried the wire-rope suspenders supporting the two decks, which were connected together by wooden trusses.

In October 1853, more than a year before the bridge was completed, the upper deck was leased to the Great Western Railway of Canada. The finished deck had a single track with four rails to accommodate the different gauges of the New York Central, the Great Western, and the Canandaigua & Niagara Falls Railroad, which were 4 feet 8½ inches, 5 feet 6 inches, and 6 feet respectively. Roebling himself had spoken in vain against the adoption of the broad gauge by the Great Western, when he appeared as an expert witness before the Railway Committee of the Province of Canada in 1851. The unfortunate choice of what became known as the 'Provincial' gauge virtually nullified the use of the Canadian railway as an American trunk line, as Roebling had predicted it would. In the 1860s the Great Western laid a third rail along its lines to provide a standard gauge track in addition to its broad gauge, and so avoid the expensive transhipment of freight. However, there was really no substitute for the adoption of the standard gauge of 4 feet 8½ inches, and the broad gauge was eventually abandoned. The Canandaigua & Niagara Falls was converted to standard gauge after it was taken over by the New York Central in 1857.

The first locomotive crossed the bridge on March 8, 1855, 'The Union Jack and Stars and Stripes were displayed. The engine was stopped in the centre of the bridge to give three hearty cheers, and then crossed to the American side and back.' The bridge was officially opened ten days later, when an experimental freight train of twenty loaded cars was pushed across the bridge by a 26-ton locomotive.

In May 1855 John A. Roebling submitted his final report to the directors of the Niagara Falls Suspension and Niagara Falls International Bridge Companies:

'It gives me great pleasure to be enabled to report the Niagara Suspension Rail Way Bridge complete in all its parts. The success of this work may now be considered an established fact. The trains of the New York Central, and of the Great Western Rail Road in Canada, have been crossing regularly since the 18th of March, averaging over 30 trips per day.

'One single observation of the passage of a train over the Niagara Bridge, will convince the most sceptical, that the practicability of Suspended Railway Bridges, so much doubted heretofore, has been successfully demonstrated ...

'While the European Engineers are engaged in the construction of short lines of Railways at such enormous cost, that in most cases the capital invested, yields no remunerative dividends, the task of the American Engineer is to lay down thousands of miles with extensive bridging, at a cost which would barely suffice in Great Britain to cover the expense of preliminary proceedings.

'The work which you did me the honor to entrust to my charge, has cost less than $400,000. The same object accomplished in Europe would have cost 4 millions without serving a better purpose, or insuring greater safety. The mixed application of timber and iron in connection with wire, render it possible to put up so large a work at so small a cost. When hereafter, by reason of greater wealth and increased traffic, we can afford to expend more on such Public Works, we shall construct them entirely of iron, omitting all perishable materials. We may then see Railway Bridges suspended of 2000 feet span, which will admit passage of trains at the highest speed ...

'In reporting to you the final and successful completion of the Bridge, I would be doing injustice to my own feelings as a man, if I did not avail myself of this opportunity, to thank you publicly for the unwavering confidence, which you have always placed in my professional ability. When Engineers of acknowledged talent and reputation freely expressed their doubts as to the success of this work, a wavering of confidence on your part would have been but natural. But I am happy to state here, that in all my operations I have always met with a cordial support. It is a great satisfaction to me, that this work has turned out equal to my promise, and also to know, that on taking leave of you, the mutual confidence that exists, will not undergo any change.'

Roebling's bridge became almost as much of a tourist attraction as the Falls; a guide-book of 1857 described it as 'the greatest artificial curiosity in America'. In 1879-80 the wooden stiffening trusses, which had deteriorated over the years, were replaced with steel, and a number of other alterations made which increased the effective strength of the bridge. At the same time the bridge was stripped of 'all superfluous material, as cornices, the rails forming the broad gauge track, &c., in all decreasing the weight about 80 tons.' In 1886 the stone towers of the bridge were replaced by iron towers, Ten years later the continually increasing weight of railway traffic made it necessary to replace the suspension span with a steel arch, which was erected around the original bridge in such a way that there was no interference with traffic during construction. Like Roebling's bridge, the steel arch bridge, completed in 1897 and still in use today, carries railway tracks on its upper deck and road traffic on its lower deck.

Roebling's bridge was an important link between the expanding American and Canadian railways, but it did not enable the Great Western to secure a significant portion of the traffic between the east and west of the northern United States. Even if the Canadian railway had not foolishly adopted the 'Provincial' gauge, any hopes of the long-sought American trade materializing were dashed by the effectiveness of the Erie Canal and the American network of railways with their termini at Buffalo. The expansion of the communities on both sides of the Niagara River was almost halted. Until the last decades of the nineteenth century and the large-scale development of hydraulic power, none of these communities was much more than a village.

A

Terminus of the Erie Canal at Buffalo
From Captain Basil Hall's
Forty etchings,
from sketches made with the camera lucida,
in North America, in 1827 and 1828

B

Account of the schooner *Amelia*
with Porter, Barton & Co., 1811-14
Buffalo & Erie County Historical Society

C

Map by Horatio A. Parsons, 1836
Although this map has a few small errors –
Fort George, for example,
is shown in the location of Fort Mississauga,
a later fort completed after the War of 1812 –
it is the best map of the Niagara River and its environs
in the 1830s
before the building of the first railways.

D

Buffalo Republican Extra
3 December 1829
Ontario Archives

E

'Ship Canal around the Falls of the Niagara'
Coloured engraving, c. 1836
Smithsonian Institution

F

Bank-note of
The Niagara Suspension Bridge Bank, 1840

G

Stock certificate
of the Buffalo & Niagara Falls Railroad, *c.* 1850

H

Roebling's Niagara Suspension Bridge
Photograph by William England, 1859

I

Train on the Suspension Bridge
Photograph by William England, 1859
Museum of Modern Art

J

Handbill of the Erie & Ontario Railway, 1858

K

John Augustus Roebling
Engraving from his
Long and short span railway bridges, 1869
Smithsonian Institution

L

Upper deck of the Suspension Bridge
From a stereograph by Charles Bierstadt
c. 1870

M

Steel arch bridge under construction, 1897
Smithsonian Institution
A freight train can be seen on the cantilever bridge
of the Michigan Central Railroad
a few hundred feet upstream.
This wrought iron and steel bridge,
built in 1883 by Charles C. Schneider,
made engineering history
when it was erected in the short time of eight months.
In 1925 it too was replaced by a steel arch bridge.

VII

BUFFALO ON LAKE ERIE.

A

Dr. Schooner America own'd by D Bea[rd]

1811 Jany. 21	To 1 Barrel Salt fr. Israel Taylor pr. D Beard's directions	6. 00	
	To 6 " do deficient in Cargo Ship'd 21 Sept.	36. —	
April 17	To 70 " do del. Capt. J Beard — 6 —	—	
	To 58 " do it being part of 130 Barrels Ship'd 30th of Octobr 1810 – Consign'd to D Beard + the remaining 72 Bls having been applied to use of A. Porter as appears by the Account of W Beard	6.00	
24	To 45 " do Cong. to J Woolverton Esq	6.75	
Nov. 1	To fr. of 70 Bls Salt to Detroit in April 1811	1.50	
4	To 118 Bls. Salt. Ship'd & Cong'd to D Beard 6. —		
	To fr. 118 " Do —	1. 50	
			$ 21
1814 Nov 4	To a Credit for Pitch & Rosin which belongs to the account of 1811		
			21
	To amount of Credits now put to the Credit of David Beard to settle this account		22
			$ 43.

Canandaigua Nov[ember] ...
the Books of Porter Barton ...
pr Count — Errors & om[issions] ...

PETER A. PORTER COLLECTION

B

K-61

n Sibley – in Account with Porter Barton & Co — Cr.

By freights of 2479 Barrels Salt from Black Rock
to Erie in season of 1810 @ .75 ——— 1859.25
By Carrying up the rapid 321 Bls @ .6 — 19.26
Payable in Salt at 6 Dolls. at B Rock ——— 1878 51
By Pitch & Rosin — ——— 1 25
By A. Porter for frt. of 72 Bls. Salt to Detroit
in November 1810 — — 1.50 — 108
By 30 Bls Salt part of 118 Bls. Ship'd 4th Nov. relanded
to make Room for Goods — — — 7.50 225 —
Nov 4. 1814 N.B. David Beard has Credit for other freights $ 2212 76
done in Nov 1810 for A. Porter – which ought to have been
in this account – but in the present State of the accounts
the entries are left to stand as they were made – it makes
no difference to either party in the result. N. Sill
See Black Rock Day Book page 363. ———
By frt. 1 Ton Iron — 2.91
" 6 Bls Whisky — 2.66 in 1810 from your Book — 5 57
2218 33

By amount of debit now Charg'd D. Beard }
to Balance this Account ——— } — — 2105 —
$ 4323 33

814 Examined – and Compar'd with
Black Rock by N. Sill & found to
ted — N. Sill – for late firm of
Porter Barton & Co

frt. alluded to in the above note —
PB&Co: 20 Bls whisky — 12/
2 " Sundries — "
3 " Rosin — "
1 Keg — — 4/ —
Ship'd 30 Oct. 1810 Cons'd to D Beard Detroit
for & on acct. of A. Porter ~~Contractor~~

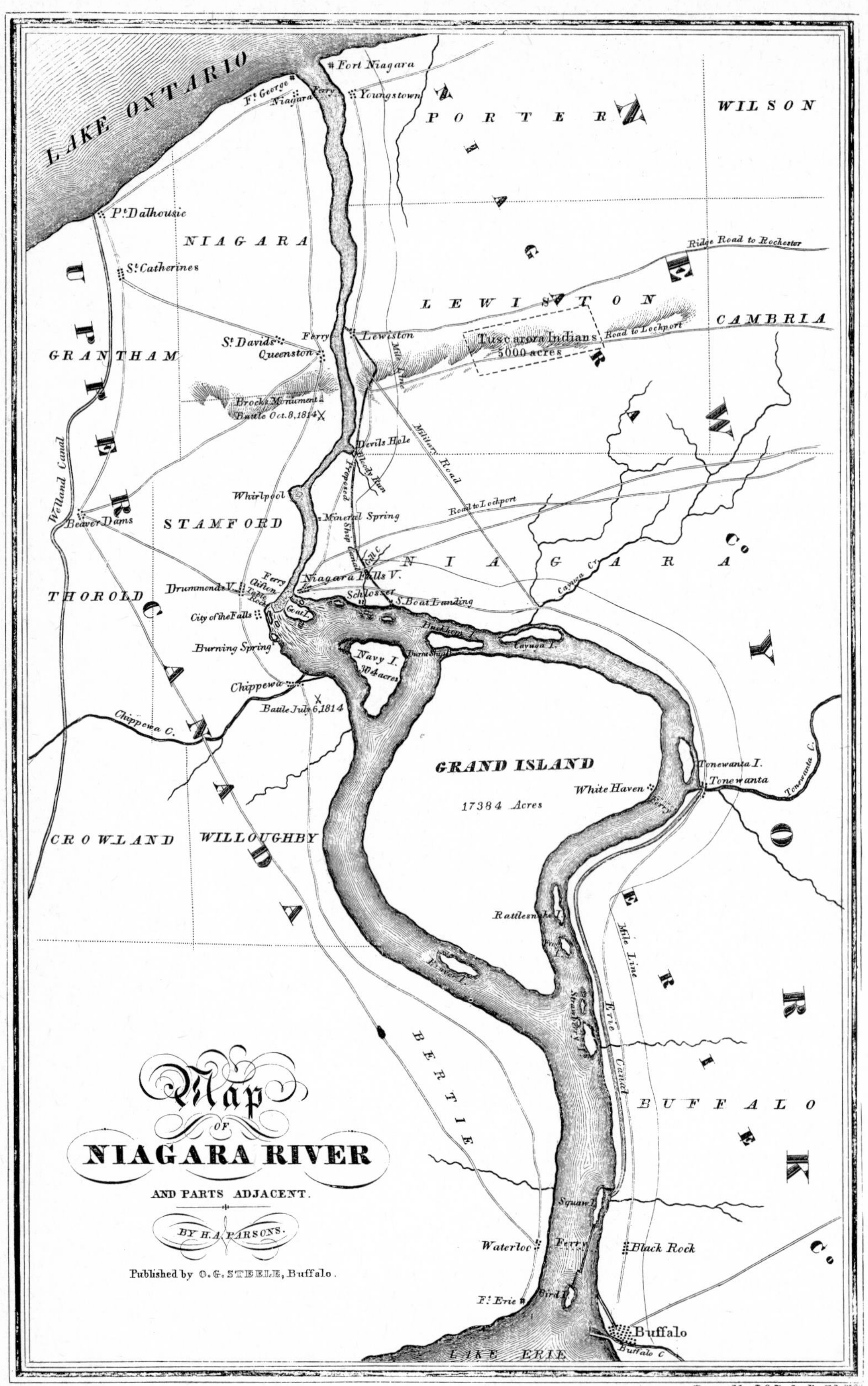

Engraved by J. G. Darby, Buffalo N.Y.

C

Buffalo Republican Extra, Dec. 3d, 1829.

The first vessels from Lake Ontario. To the surprise of the citizens of Buffalo and Black Rock, the Lake Schooners Ann & Jane of York, U. C. and R. H. Boughton of Youngstown, arrived in our harbor, on Wednesday last, having on board the enterprizing projector of the Welland Canal, *William Hamilton Merritt*, with a company of gentlemen, (whose names the subjoined certificates disclose.) The British vessel led the van. The Locks were passed on the 30th of Novem'r, just five years from the commencement of the important work. The question is not, whether this work will increase or diminish the receipts of the Erie canal,—we trust that we possess too much national pride, to complain of the success of even a rival work, began by our neighbors before ours was completed. Its progress to its termination, is now flattering, and the news we now communicate, that of *the passage of vessels from Lake to Lake*, surmounting the declivity which causes the fall of the Niagara, must be cheering indeed to the stockholders, and gratifying to the inhabitants of Upper Canada.

Both vessels passed into the Black Rock basin through the sloop-lock, and were saluted by the Steamboat Henry Clay, and cheered by the citizens. On their arrival in our harbor, they were met with bursts of applause, and honored by discharges of artillery from the terrace. The gentlemen passengers then repaired to the Eagle Tavern, where they were greeted by many of our villagers, who called to shake the hand of the navigators of the Deep Cut!

The passage of the first vessels was to have taken effect, by a notification of the W.C.C. Directors 24th ult.; but, owing to the storms, and unfavorable state of the weather, was postponed. The zeal of the projector and persevering agent, could not be satisfied with a " postponement on account of the weather," so he and the gentlemen who accompanied him, made the attempt; and, after cutting ice, in some places three inches thick; ascending thirty-two locks, at the mountain; passing the deepest of all " cuts;" locking down into the Welland river; sailing down that river, and touching at Chippewa; stemming the strong and broad current of the Niagara; and, finally, the Black Rock harbor, which has been blamed beyond measure, opened its arms and gave the " tars from Ontario" a glorious hug.

The success of our neighbors may give an impetus to our national or state governments, or a body corporate, in making a canal or rail-way, from the Niagara river at Schlosser, to the same river, at Lewiston.

Truly, the bold features of the enterprizes of the New World, throw those of the Old, far in the shade.

[CERTIFICATES.]

District of Niagara, Port of Youngstown.

This is to certify, that Isaac T. Pheatt, master of the Schr. R. H. Boughton, bound for Buffalo, having on board passengers, baggage and sea-stores, has regularly entered and cleared his said vessel according to law. Given under my hand, &c.

(Signed) A. G. HINMAN,
Dep'y Coll'r Youngstown.

Port of Chippewa, ss.

This is to certify, that the British Schr. Ann & Jane, bound from York to Buffalo, Joseph Vollor, master, and the American Schr. R.H. Boughton, I. T. Pheatt, master, both arrived in this port, on the evening of this day, and severally made reports of their entry and clearance.

ROB. KIRKPATRICK,
30th Nov 1829. Collector.

This is to certify, to all whom it may concern, that I left the port of Youngstown, on Lake Ontario, in the Schr. R. H. Boughton, a standing keel vessel, burthen equal to 85 tons British measurement, on the 26th November,—passed through the Welland Canal, and arrived at Buffalo, on the 2d December, instant. We passed all the locks, 32 in number, from Lake Ontario to the summit of the mountain in 5 1-2 hours, without the least delay or impediment; and I have not the least doubt, on the completion of the towing path on the Welland River, that a vessel will pass from Lake Ontario to Lake Erie in twenty four hours.

(Signed,) I. T. PHEATT, mast'r.
Port of Buffalo, Lake Erie,
2d Dec. 1829.

We, the undersigned, gentlemen passengers, on board the above-named Schooner, from Youngstown to Buffalo, believe the above statement to be correct.

(Signed) *And. Estes*, *Geo. Barber*,
Sam'l M. Chubbuck, *O. Hathaway*.

This is to certify, that the Schr. Ann & Jane, left the port of York, on Lake Ontario, on the 25th November; passed thro' the Welland Canal, and arrived at the port of Fort Erie, on 2d December instant; and that I have no doubt that the passage thro' the whole line of the Welland Canal from Lake Ontario to Lake Erie, can hereafter be effected in the course of 24 hours.

(Signed) JOSEPH VOLLOR,
Port of Fort Erie, 2d Dec. 1829. Master.

We, the undermentioned gentlemen, came passengers in the British Schooner Ann and Jane, and the American Schooner R. H. Boughton, from various parts of the Welland Canal; and have no doubt, from the statement of those who passed through the whole line, as well as from our own observation, that vessels will hereafter, pass from Lake Ontario to Lake Erie through the Welland Canal within 24 hours. (Signed,)

Robert Randall, M. P. P.
John J. Lefferty, M. P. P. } Directors of the W. Canal Company.
George Keefer,
Samuel Street, J. W. Garrison,
Wm. A. Campbell, David Wm. Smith,
James Little, Jacob Ditterick,
Jacob Keefer, John Haiver.

THIS VIEW OF THE SHIP CANAL AROUND THE FALLS OF THE NIAGARA

is Dedicated with the utmost respect and esteem to LIEUT. COL. JOHN J. ABERT,

Chief of the Corps of U.S. TOP. ENGINEERS, *by his obedient Servant*

W. G. Williams Capt. U.S. Top. Engineers

E

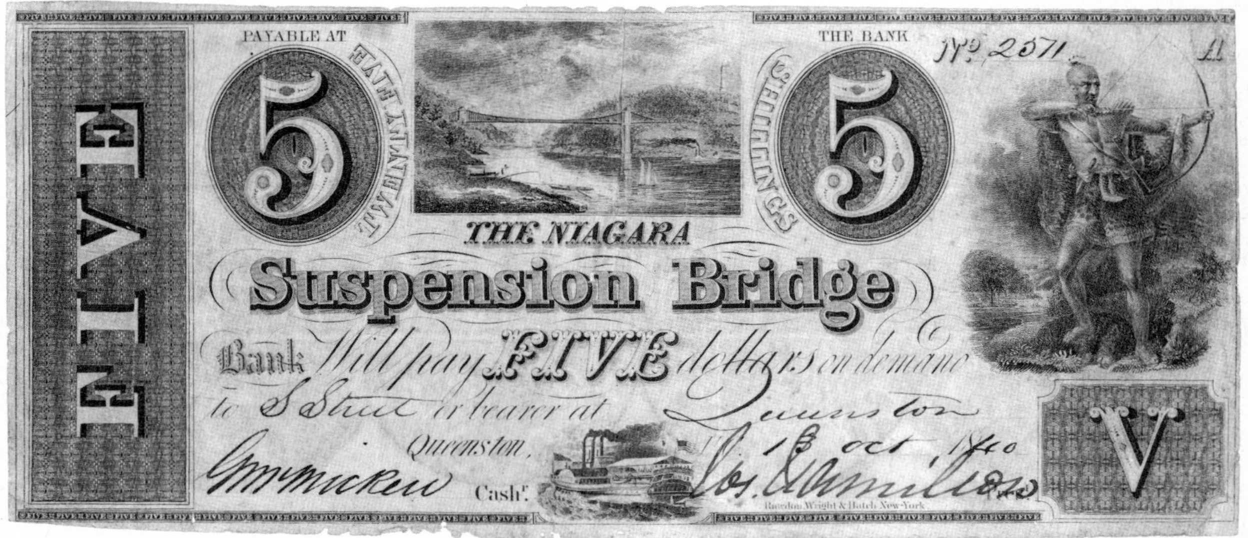

FIVE
PAYABLE AT
THE BANK
No. 2571
5
TWENTY FIVE
SHILLINGS
5
THE NIAGARA
Suspension Bridge
Bank Will pay FIVE dollars on demand
to S Street or bearer at Queenston
Queenston,
Cash.r
V
Rawdon, Wright & Hatch New-York

F

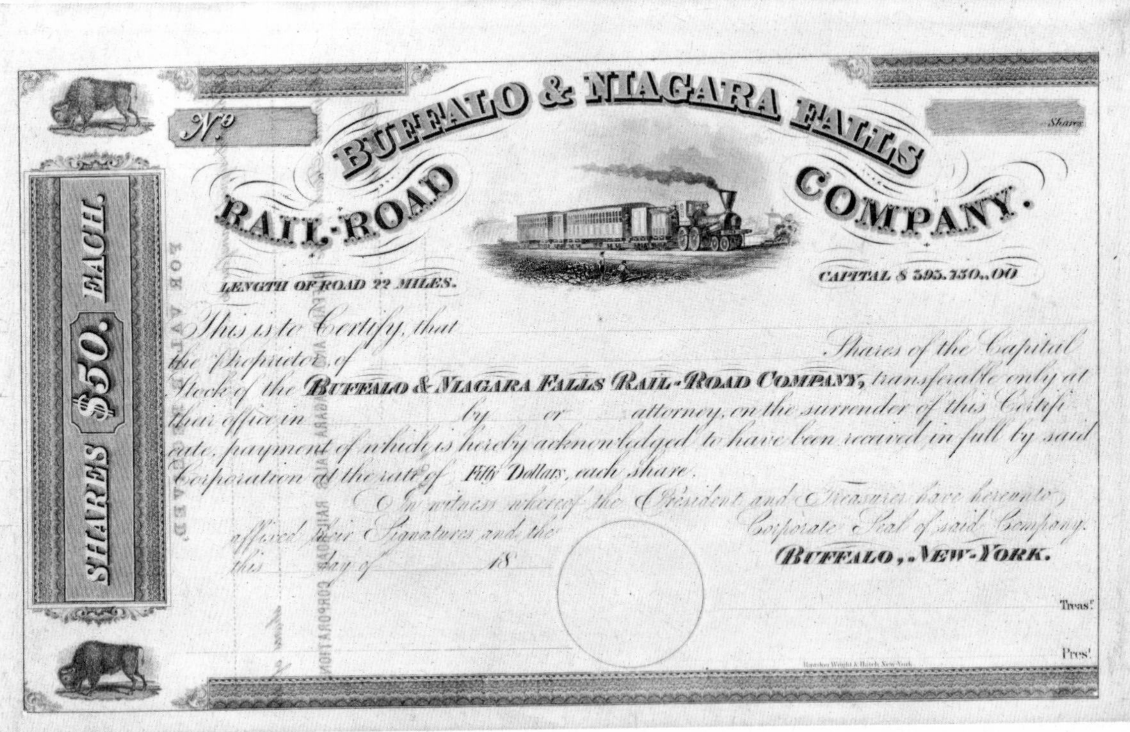

No.

Shares

BUFFALO & NIAGARA FALLS RAIL-ROAD COMPANY.

LENGTH OF ROAD 22 MILES.

CAPITAL $ 595.450,,00

SHARES $50. EACH.

This is to Certify, that the Proprietor of Shares of the Capital Stock of the BUFFALO & NIAGARA FALLS RAIL-ROAD COMPANY, transferable only at their office in by or attorney, on the surrender of this Certificate, payment of which is hereby acknowledged to have been received in full by said Corporation at the rate of Fifty Dollars, each share.

In witness whereof the President and Treasurer have hereunto affixed their Signatures and the Corporate Seal of said Company this day of 18

BUFFALO,, NEW-YORK.

Treas.r

Pres.t

G

H

1858. SUMMER ARRANGEMENT. 1858.

ERIE & ONTARIO RAILWAY.

TIME-TABLE.

BETWEEN NIAGARA, SUSPENSION BRIDGE AND CHIPPAWA.

ON and after MONDAY, the 17th MAY, 1858, and until further notice, (Sunday's excepted), Trains will run as follows :—

STATIONS.	Going South.	*STATIONS.*	Going North.
			A. M.
Leave NIAGARA,.................	A. M.	*Leave* CHIPPAWA,.................	11.15
(on arrival of Boat from Toronto).	10.00	CLIFTON HOUSE,..........	11.25
QUEENSTON,..............	10.15	SUS. BRIDGE..............	11.35
STAMFORD,................	10.25	STAMFORD................	11.50
SUS. BRIDGE,.............	10.40	QUEENSTON...............	12.00
CLIFTON HOUSE,..........	10.50	*Arrive* NIAGARA..............	
Arrive CHIPPAWA,...............	11.00	(Connecting with boat for Toronto.)	12.15

CONNECTIONS GOING SOUTH.

At Suspension Bridge with Great Western Railway, and with N. Y. Central Railroad, East, and for Buffalo.

CONNECTIONS GOING NORTH.

At Suspension Bridge with the Great Western, and N. Y. Central Railways, arriving at Niagara in time for

STEAMER PEERLESS,

For Toronto, connecting there with the Grand Trunk Railroad and Royal Mail Line of Steamers for Montreal.

FARE FROM BUFFALO TO TORONTO, - - - - $2.00.
SUS. BRIDGE, " - - - - - 1.50.

J. B. ROBERTSON,

Lessee.

NIAGARA, May 14th 1858.

K

L

M

STUNTERS

In the nineteenth century Niagara became an arena for stunts. The first of these was a singularly cruel and pointless spectacle. In September 1827, a partially dismantled schooner, the *Michigan*, was sent over the Falls with a cargo of animals on board. William Lyon Mackenzie, then editor and publisher of the *Colonial Advocate*, travelled from Toronto with his family to report on the incident.

'The day was very favourable, and every steamboat, schooner, and stage coach, which could be procured within many miles of the Falls were in motion, as well as waggons and other vehicles beyond calculation – the roads to the Falls in every direction were like the approaches to Yorkshire fair, and perhaps there were eight or ten thousand persons on the spot by one o'clock P.M. including show men with wild beasts, gingerbread people, cake and beer stalls, wheel of fortune men, &c.

'The two hotels and the galleries were crowded with people dressed in the pink of fashion;–the banks of the river above and below Goat Island–the British and American shores–trees–houses & house-tops–on waggons & waggon wheels–every place and every corner and nook was filled with human beings–bands of music enlivened the scene;–and the roar of the African Lion in the menagerie, and the din of the passing multitude, joined to the crash of the cataract, were almost too much for human organs.'

The event itself was somewhat of a fiasco, since the ship broke up before it reached the brink of the Falls – by which time some of the animals had escaped. Nevertheless, as Mackenzie wrote, 'the tavern-keepers cleared a great deal of money by the transaction'.

Two years later a 'blasting-off fête' was proposed. Sir John Colborne, Lieutenant-Governor of Upper Canada, had given permission to William Forsyth, proprietor of The Pavilion hotel, to blow up part of Table Rock that had become unsafe. The explosion did not take place; instead Sam Patch made the first of his two leaps into the Niagara River from a special platform built out from Goat Island.

'On Wednesday the 7th inst. [7 October 1829]', the *Colonial Advocate* reported, 'the celebrated SAM PATCH actually leaped over the Falls of Niagara into the vast abyss below. A ladder was projected from Goat Island about 40 feet down, on which Sam walked out clad in white, and with great deliberation put his hands close to his sides and jumped from the platform ... While the boats below were on the look-out for him, he had in one minute reached the shore unnoticed and unhurt, and was heard on the beach singing as merrily as if altogether unconscious of having performed an act so extraordinary as almost to appear an incredible fable. Sam Patch has immortalised himself – he has done what mortal never did before – he has precipitated himself eighty-five feet in one leap; that leap into the mighty cavern of Niagara's Cataract; and survives the romantic feat uninjured!!!'

Sam Patch had already become a national celebrity when he jumped into the Passaic River in 1827. Shortly after his two successful jumps at Niagara, he drowned after leaping into the Genesee River at Rochester, N.Y.

Sam Patch passed into American folklore; later, Jean François Gravelet, better known as Blondin, was to achieve world-wide fame with his exploits at Niagara. Blondin had intended to walk from the Terrapin Rocks over the Horseshoe Falls to the Canadian shore, but the Porter family, the owners of Goat Island, refused to give their permission for this perilous stunt, and so his tightrope was stretched across the Gorge about three-quarters of a mile below the Falls. The Toronto *Globe* reported that more than ten thousand people viewed his first performance on June 30, 1859.

'Precisely at a quarter to five o'clock he seized his balancing pole, weighing about fifty pounds, and although the sun was shining in his eyes, he tripped forward, and almost before the people were aware he had cleared the American land, and nothing intervened between him and destruction but a two-inch rope. The bands struck lively airs, and the spectators on the Canada shore were about to greet the daring adventurer with a cheer, when they were stilled by the men in Blondin's employ. Blondin marched on at a lively pace, his toes hardly appearing to touch the rope. After walking out about 150 yards, he suddenly sank down on the rope and took a short rest. An involuntary shudder passed through the crowd as he thus fearlessly threw himself on his face on the cable, while several of the ladies gave a *petite* scream, and clung more firmly to their protectors ...

'On arriving about a third of the distance across, Blondin sat down once more, and waved his hand for the *Maid of the Mist* to steam up under the rope. It had been found impossible to anchor this craft at the point assigned for her, owing to the strength of the current. After a delay of about five minutes, the steamer was brought directly underneath the rope, and by her paddles being set in motion and her head up the stream, she was kept almost stationary. Blondin then, from his giddy elevation, lowered a piece of twine, which fell on the deck of the steamer, and a bottle containing some liquor was fastened to it, which Blondin drew up, and having drank of the liquor, he tossed the bottle into the river, and in a twinkling was pursuing his perilous journey ...

'The steep ascent to the Canadian shore was the next difficulty in the way, but without stopping, Blondin nerved himself for the task. His countenance was more plainly observable from the Canadian side, and the perspiration standing on his brow indicated that he felt fatigued. His step grew slower, and a feeling began to prevail that he might even yet fail in the attempt to reach the now nearly-won goal. Not a face in the vast crowd which did not wear an anxious look. There was a death-like stillness, and with "bated breath" the spectators gazed upon Blondin as he ascended the rope. A few seconds elapsed, and then the deep silence gave place to a tremendous shout, which announced that Blondin had succeeded in crossing the River on a rope so slender that to the on-lookers that it appeared but littler stouter than a spider's web.'

Blondin gave his second performance on July 4, and followed it with further performances during the summer of 1859. His acrobatic feats on the tight-rope astounded the world, most particularly when on August 17 he carried his manager, Harry Colcord, across on his back. Blondin returned to Niagara the following year, when his rope was stretched across the whirlpool rapids downstream from the suspension bridge.

This year a 'new candidate' for fame, Signor Farini, actually a William Leonard Hunt, born at Lockport, N.Y., had his rope close to the Falls. The *Globe* gave an account of Farini's first performance on August 15, 1860.

'After advancing very slowly a short distance down the rope he reached the first guy, where he reclined on his back for a short period. He then rose to his feet and moved nimbly forward a fourth part of the distance, where he rested his pole on the guy ropes and commenced his acrobatic performance, which consisted of standing on his head, hanging by his hands and feet, and reclining on his back. He reached the Canadian shore forty minutes after starting from the American side, apparently a good deal fatigued, and was well received by the spectators. On his return trip he descended by a rope to the deck of the steamer *Maid of the Mist*, but not head foremost as had been announced. He then ascended to the cable after performing some feats on the perpendicular rope, and reached the American shore in safety. He is not quite so active on the rope as Mons. Blondin, but he will no doubt improve by practice.'

On August 28, 1860, the *Globe* carried an advertisement headed 'TREMENDOUS EXCITEMENT!' It announced a 'grand excursion' the next day to Niagara Falls, where 'both MONSIEUR BLONDIN AND SIGNOR FARINI will walk their ropes WITH MEN ON THEIR BACKS, and also give two GRAND MOONLIGHT ASCENSIONS'. Blondin repeated his performance of the previous year and carried Harry Colcord, while Farini carried a Rowland McMullen.

The world-wide interest in Blondin's feats made Niagara a magnet for tightrope performers, and Farini was only one of many to repeat the Frenchman's daring. But neither Farini nor any of the others achieved Blondin's fame. A 'Professor' Jenkins tried an unusual variation; the *Niagara Falls Gazette* of September 1, 1869, stated:

'We have been pretty reticent in regard to the proposition of Jenkins – the "Canadian Blondin" – to cross the Niagara on a velocipede. Somehow there appeared an air of humbug about the fellow, and our suspicions have been realized.

'The "great feat" came off last Wednesday, and a good many spectators were pretty well Jenkinsized. His velocipede was just no velocipede at all but a sort of machine so attached to the rope that it could not fall, and the rider was reasonably secure from accident. The "feat" was about equal to that of the son of Erin who runs a hand-car.

'Jenkins's performance bears about as much resemblance to Blondin's as a poor counterfeit does to the genuine. If our Canadian neighbours can't turn out better performers than this one they had better keep them for some more useful purpose.'

When Henry Bellini arrived at the Falls in 1873 there was 'considerable apathy', according to the *Niagara Falls Gazette*, towards his 'prospective exhibition of funambulistic skill, owing, in part, to the fact that the feasibility of the undertaking had already been abundantly proved'. However, the newspaper was considerably impressed when Bellini made his 'couchone leap' from the tightrope in to the Niagara River. For this feat he had a rubber cord, twelve feet long and an inch and a quarter in diameter, fastened to the tightrope. A short handle-bar was attached to the other end of the cord.

'After adjusting his rubber attachment the fearless fellow dropped from the rope retaining the end of the rubber line in his hands until nearly to the surface of the water. His fall was very swift though, of course, his descent was somewhat retarded by the precautionary contrivance, which sprang upward to the rope the instant he released it. Going under the water for an instant, he quickly rose to the surface and was taken into a boat in waiting for him and rowed to the Canada shore where his wife was waiting to meet him.'

Bellini repeated his leap a few days later, but when he attempted it a third time, the rubber cord parted from the tightrope and he fell into the river with the cord wound around his legs. He was lucky enough to be picked up before he drowned, and afterwards announced that he would not attempt the leap again 'as the water was several degrees to[o] cold for comfort or safety'.

Stephen Peer, a young man from nearby Drummondville, Ontario, was employed as an assistant by Bellini. Peer tried to obtain permission from the authorities to use the rope and, according to the *Gazette*, 'finally secured permission to *land* in Prospect Park, but was forbidden *starting* from this side on his perilous trip. Borrowing Balleni's balancing-pole the amateur funambulist started out from the Canada shore on *a positive trot*. During the trip across he stopped and went through with many of Blondin's most difficult acrobatic and gymnastic feats, astonishing not only spectators generally but also his friends by the ease, grace and skill with which he acquitted himself'. Peer gave further performances on the tightrope, at which Bellini became so insanely jealous that he tried to cut the rope. His attempt 'excited intense indignation among those cognizant of the deed, imperilling as it did the life of his intrepid rival, who could not be warned in time to prevent his crossing the dangerous rope'. Fourteen years later, in 1887, Peer performed on a rope between the two railway bridges. Three days afterwards he was found dead under the Canadian end of the cable – it is thought that he tried to walk across at night when he was drunk.

Maria Spelterini was the only woman to perform on a tightrope at Niagara. The *Niagara Falls Gazette* reporting on her first exhibition, which took place on July 8, 1876, wrote: 'The Signorina made the cross and return trips attired in flesh colored tights, a tunic of scarlet, a sea-green boddice, and neat green buskins. The lady is twenty-three years of age, with dark Italian features, superbly built, and weighing close in the neighbourhood of a hundred and fifty pounds. She made no attempt to walk against time, merely travelling the gossamer web with a graceful, confident step, which soon allayed all apprehension of impeding disaster.'

Maria Spelterini apparently came to Niagara to establish her fame in North America before visiting the Centennial Exhibition at Philadelphia. She was much photographed, and more than one stereograph was published of her crossing with baskets on her feet.

Not one of the many tightrope-walkers lost his life at Niagara with the exception of Peer, whose death seems to have been accidental, but on July 24, 1883, Captain Matthew Webb, the first man to swim the English Channel, drowned in an attempt to swim the rapids below the Falls. The *Saturday Review* expressed the general European attitude towards his disastrous stunt:

'It was unquestionably very appropriate that Mr. Webb should have met his death in America, and in sight of the United States. That country has a passion for big shows, and has now been indulged in the biggest thing of its kind which has been seen in this generation. Nothing was to be gained by success – if success had been possible – beyond a temporary notoriety and the applause of a mob ...

'As long as there is a popular demand for these essentially barbarous amusements, men and women will be found who are desperate, or greedy, or vain enough to risk their lives and ruin their health for money or applause ... The death of Mr. Webb is shocking in the last degree; but it will not be wholly useless if it at least awakens the sight-seeing world to some sense of what it is they have been encouraging.'

In fact, however, Webb's death encouraged rather than deterred other notoriety-seekers. A new era, that of the 'barrel-cranks', began in 1886 when Carlisle D. Graham, a Philadelphia cooper, made a successful trip through the rapids in a wooden cask. Graham made a number of similar trips and became known as the 'Hero of Whirlpool Rapids'. Others made the journey safely in both barrels and specially constructed boats. Some were not so fortunate; in 1888 Robert Flack died in a boat supposedly made safe with a 'secret filling' – excelsior and wood shavings – and in 1901 Maud Willard was killed using Graham's barrel.

The rapids lost their glamour when on October 24, 1901, Mrs. Anna Edson Taylor went over the Horseshoe Falls in a barrel. Her barrel finally grounded on a rock near the shore, and a portion of the top had to be sawn off before she could be helped out. She was bleeding from a cut on her head, but was otherwise uninjured although suffering from bruises and shock. Mrs. Taylor told reporters that she was a widow, forty-three years old, and that the sole purpose of her feat was to make money. Her dreams of a successful lecture-tour never materialized; people were not interested in an unattractive, middle-aged woman who had nothing to offer but her foolhardiness. She returned to Niagara Falls, where she sat in the street beside a fake barrel – her original one had been left in the water and had rotted – and sold autographed postcards. She died in 1921, a pauper. Six others have followed her example and gone over the Falls in one sort of contraption or another; three of them have been killed.

In his book *The Niagara River* published in 1908, Archer Butler Hulbert wrote:

'Graham's performances, possibly, were also of some practical value. It was proven to the observant that a particular shape of cask might, under certain conditions, be used to draw feeble or sickly passengers from a wrecked ship in bad weather, for a woman or child could have lived in Graham's machine as well as the cooper himself; however, the circumstances are few under which it would be useful, and Graham, by his own account, had no idea of applying his contrivance in any such way.'

Hulbert's attempt to provide some justification for Graham is hardly convincing, and the feats of the barrel-cranks have only added to the tawdry reputation of Niagara.

At the International Carnival of 1911, Lincoln Beachey, one of the greatest of the early stunt pilots, revived the daring and professionalism of the tightrope-walkers when he flew under the Falls View Bridge. In an account published the following day (28 June 1911) the *Niagara Falls Gazette* quotes Beachey as saying:

'For a portion of the trip my eyes were shut and I cannot now remember whether they were shut or open when I went under the bridge. But I do know this. I dropped so fast that the flow of gasoline was stopped and the engine missed several times. That has happened with me before, but never in such a dangerous place. The spray from the falls cut my face like a knife and struck my eyes so I had to shut them.

'It was just under the bridge that the machine seemed to go down and down, as though it was in a vacuum. The space under the bridge seemed awfully small when I was down there in the river. I was close to the Canadian side because the air currents from the American Falls drove me over that way. I wanted to pass under the center of the bridge. There was between six and twenty feet between the top plane and the arch of the bridge, and I was probably twenty feet above the water.'

Beachey's flight in a Curtiss biplane is almost forgotten today. So too are the performances of the many tightrope-walkers at Niagara. Ironically, the stunts of the dull, notoriety-seeking barrel-cranks, particularly of the twentieth century, have gained at least a local reputation.

A

Poster advertising the descent of the *Michigan*, 1827
Buffalo & Erie County Historical Society

B

Advertisement of Sam Patch
From the *Colonial Advocate*, 15 October 1829
Ontario Archives
This advertisement has been reproduced
from Mackenzie's own copy of his newspaper.
The 'X' was to inform the printer
that it was to be removed from the next issue.

C

'Blondin March': music cover, 1861
The New-York Historical Society

D

Blondin carrying Colcord
From a stereograph by Platt D. Babbitt, 17 August 1859

E

Poster advertising Blondin's performance on July 4, 1859
Buffalo & Erie County Historical Society

F

Punch cartoon, 8 October 1859
Lord Palmerston, the prime minister,
wheels Lord John Russell, the foreign secretary,
over a rope labelled 'Palmerstonian Politics'.

G

'Blondin's tight-rope Feat –
Spectators viewing his Performance'
From a stereograph by William England, 1859

H

Farini, from a stereograph by Platt D. Babbitt, 1860

I

Farini 'in his wonderful and laughable character of Biddy O'Flaherty the Irish washerwoman', from a stereograph by Platt D. Babbitt
On September 5, 1860, Farini gave a special performance to advertise a patent washing machine. When he was in the middle of the rope, he drew up a pail of water from the river and proceeded to wash the handkerchiefs given to him by several ladies. 'It was a difficult performance,' the *Niagara Falls Gazette* reported, 'but it was done well.'

J

'Professor' Jenkins, from a stereograph by Charles Bierstadt, 1869

K

Bellini's 'couchone leap', from a faked stereograph by George Barker, 1873

L

Stephen Peer, from a stereograph by George Barker, 1873

M

Maria Spelterini, from a stereograph by George E. Curtis, 1876

N

Maria Spelterini, from a stereograph probably by Charles Bierstadt, 1876

O

'Graham, The Hero of Whirlpool Rapids, and his Barrel'
Photograph by George Barker, 1886. *Buffalo & Erie County Historical Society*

P

Captain Webb: an embossed scrapbook print, *c.* 1883

Q

Mrs. Taylor, from a stereograph, 24 October 1901. *Library of Congress*

R

Lincoln Beachey flying under the Falls View Bridge
From a faked photograph, 1911. *Library of Congress*

S

Promotional envelope for the International Carnival, 1911.

The Pirate, MICHIGAN,

WITH A CARGO OF FEROCIOUS ANIMALS, WILL PASS THE GREAT RAPIDS AND THE FALLS OF

NIAGARA,

8TH SEPTEMBER, 1827, AT 3 O'CLOCK.

THE first passage of a vessel of the largest class which sails on Erie and the Upper Lakes, through the Great Rapids, and over the stupendous precipice at Niagara Falls, it is proposed to effect, on the 8th of September next.

The *Michigan* has long braved the billows of Erie, with success, as a merchant vessel; but having been *condemned* by her owners as unfit to sail longer proudly *"above;"* her present proprietors, together with several publick spirited friends, have appointed her to convey a cargo of Living Animals of the Forests, which surround the Upper Lakes, through the white tossing, and the deep rolling rapids of the Niagara, and down its grand precipice, into the basin *"below."*

The greatest exertions are making to procure Animals of the most ferocious kind, such as Panthers, Wild Cats, Bears, and Wolves; but in lieu of some of these, which it may be impossible to obtain, a few vicious or worthless Dogs, such as may possess considerable strength and activity, and perhaps a few of the toughest of the Lesser Animals, will be added to, and compose, the cargo.

Capt. *James Rough*, of Black Rock, the oldest navigator of the Upper Lakes, has generously volunteered his services to manage this enterprise, in which he will be seconded by Mr. *Levi Allen*, mate of the Steamboat *Niagara*—the publick may rest assured that they will select none but capable assistants. The manager will proceed seasonably with experiments, to ascertain the most practicable and eligible point, from which to detach the Michigan for the Rapids.

It is intended to have the *Michigan* fitted up in the style in which she is to make her splendid but perilous descent, at *Black Rock*, where she now lies. She will be dressed as a *Pirate;* besides her *Menagerie* of Wild Animals, and probably some tame ones, it is proposed to place *a Crew* (in effigy) at proper stations on board. The Animals will be caged or otherwise secured and placed on board the *"condemned Vessel,"* on the morning of the 7th, at the Ferry, where the curious can examine her with her *'cargo,'* during the day, at a trifling expense. On the morning of the 8th, the Michigan will be towed from her position at *Black Rock*, to the foot of Navy Island, by the Steamboat *Chippewa*, from whence she will be conducted by the Manager to her last moorings. Passage can be obtained in the Michigan from *Black Rock* to *Navy Island*, at *half a Dollar* each.

Should the Vessel take her course through the *deepest of the Rapids*, it is confidently believed, that she will reach the *Horse Shoe*, unbroken; if so, she will perform her voyage, *to the water in the Gulf beneath*, which is of great depth and buoyancy, entire; *but what her fate may be, the* trial *will decide*. Should the Animals be young and hardy, and *possessed of great muscular powers*, and *joining their fate* with that of the Vessel, remain on board until she reaches the waters below, there is great probability that many of them, will *have performed the terrible jaunt, unhurt!*

Such as may survive, and be retaken, will be sent to the Museums at New York and Montreal, and some perhaps to London.

It may be proper to observe, that several Steamboats are expected to be in readiness at *Buffalo*, together with numerous Coaches, for the conveyance of Passengers down, on the morning of the 8th. Coaches will leave *Buffalo*, at 2 o'clock, on the afternoon of the 7th, for the Falls on both sides of the River, for the convenience of those who may be desirous of securing accommodations at the Falls on the 8th. Ample means for the conveyance of Visitors, will be provided at *Tonawanta*, at *Lockport*, at *Lewiston*, at *Queenston*, and at *Fort George*, to either side.

As no probable estimate can now be made, of the numbers which the proposed exhibition may bring together; great disappointments regarding the extent of our accommodations, may possibly be anticipated by some; in respect to which, we beg leave to assure our respective friends and the publick in general, that, in addition to our own, which are large, (and will on the occasion be furnished to their utmost limits,) there are other Publick Houses, besides many private ones, at which comfortable entertainment can be had, for all who may visit the Falls on the present occasion—an occasion which will for its novelty and the remarkable spectacle it will present, be unequalled in the annals of *inrernal* navigation.

August 2, 1827.

P. WHITNEY, *Keeper of Eagle Hotel, United States Falls.*

WM. FORSYTH, JOHN BROWN, } *Keepers of the* Ontario House *and* Pavilion, *Canada Falls.*

SMITH H. SALISBURY, PRINTER, BLACK ROCK.

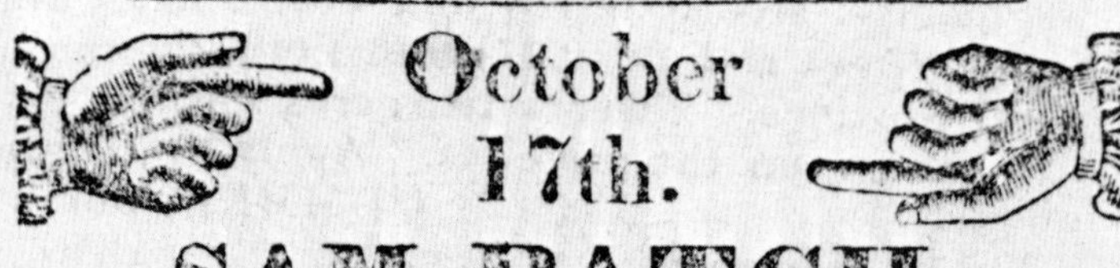

October 17th.

SAM PATCH.

To the Ladies and Gentlemen of Western New York, and of Upper Canada.

ALL I have to say is, that I arrived at the Falls too late to give you a specimen of my Jumping Qualities, on the 6th inst.; but on Wednesday, I thought I would venture a small Leap, which I accordingly made, of Eighty Feet, merely to convince those that remained to see me, with what safety and ease I could descend, and that I was the TRUE SAM PATCH, and to show that some things could be done as well as others; which was denied before I made the Jump.

Having been thus disappointed, the owners of Goat Island have generously granted me the use of it for nothing; so that I may have a chance, from an equally generous public, to obtain some remuneration for my long journey hither, as well as affording me an opportunity of supporting the reputation I have gained, by Æro-Nautical Feats, never before attempted, either in the Old or New World.

I shall Ladies and Gentlemen, on Saturday next, Oct. 17th, precisely at 3 o'clock, P. M. LEAP at the FALLS of NIAGARA, from a height of 120 to 130 feet, (being 40 to 50 feet higher than I leapt before,) into the eddy below. On my way down from Buffalo, on the morning of that day, in the Steamboat Niagara, I shall, for the amusement of the Ladies, doff my coat and spring from the mast head into the Niagara River.

SAM PATCH.
Of Passaic Falls, New-Jersey.

Buffalo, Oct. 12, 1829.

BLONDIN MARCH
to
BLONDIN
THE
HERO OF NIAGARA
BY
Albert Poppenberg
BUFFALO
Published by
BLODGETT & BRADFORD

C

D

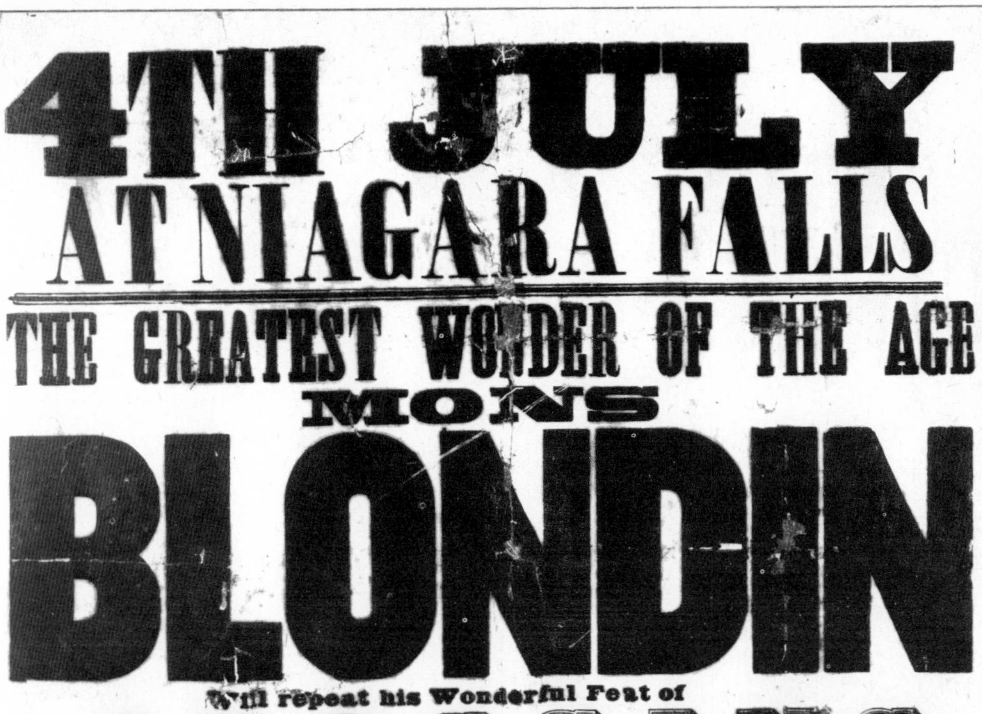

4TH JULY
AT NIAGARA FALLS

THE GREATEST WONDER OF THE AGE

MONS

BLONDIN

Will repeat his Wonderful Feat of

CROSSING

THE NIAGARA RIVER

UPON A TIGHT ROPE & RETURN

ON MONDAY

THE 4th OF JULY

Between 3 & 5 P. M. He will cross from the American Side to the Canada side

TIED UP IN A SACK

Mons. BLONDIN, will also repeat his World-Renowned Exercise on the

TIGHT ROPE!

On the Ground, previous to the Terrific and Sublime Trip across Niagara River

PRICE OF ADMISSION 25 CENTS

Splendid Seats have been erected for the occasion, price 25 Cents Extra

TIGHT ROPE Performances to begin at 3 P. M. GENERAL ASCENSION at 4 P. M

E

BLONDIN OUTDONE.

G

H

J

K

L

M N

O

CAPTAIN WEBB's LAST MOMENT IN THE NIAGARA WHIRLPOOL.

SIX MILES
OF
HISTORICAL, INDUSTRIAL
AND
PANTOMIMIC PAGEANTRY.
A MAGNIFICENT ILLUMINATION
OF THE FALLS OF NIAGARA.
GRAND INTERNATIONAL
MILITARY FEATURES.
NIAGARA'S INTERNATIONAL
CARNIVAL
THIS SPACE FOR ADDRESS.
2
DAYS
JUNE 27-28
1911
RETURN TO
NIAGARA FALLS.
NIAGARA FALLS, N.Y. U.S.A. – NIAGARA FALLS ONT. CANADA.

TOURISTS

'I am much surprised that a place so celebrated as the Falls of Niagara, and which is visited by so many travellers, amongst whom are no inconsiderable number of ladies, should not yet have induced some enterprising person to erect a convenient house on this [American] side of the river for their accommodation ...' wrote Christian Schultz, who visited Niagara in 1807. 'Judge P[orter] who owns the lands adjoining the falls on this side of the river, informed me he should, as soon as possible ... appoint some proper person to keep a genteel tavern for the accommodation of the curious.' A log tavern, built prior to the War of 1812, was one of the few buildings saved when the village, then known as Manchester, was put to the torch by the British in 1813. After the war, Parkhurst Whitney, who had been a brigadier-general in the state militia, repaired and enlarged the old, log building and gave it the name of Eagle Tavern.

'Much company at the Falls this day', Major Delafield noted in his diary for June 22, 1819. 'The accommodations miserable, otherwise travellers would be induced to remain some days at this place. Whitney the landlord is an obliging man but he & his wife entirely ignorant of either comforts or propriety in house keeping.' Nevertheless General Whitney became the most famous hotel-keeper at Niagara. In 1830 he bought the Cataract House, which, with its cupola, was a landmark for a hundred and twenty years until it was destroyed by fire in 1945.

Niagara became part of the 'fashionable tour' – the title of a little guidebook published in 1822, and the first to mention the Falls. Charles Waterton, the eccentric English naturalist, wrote after his visit in 1824 that 'words can hardly do justice to the unaffected ease and elegance of the American ladies who visit the falls of Niagara'. Waterton was greatly attracted to a young lady from Albany, who 'entered the ball-room with such becoming air and grace, that it was impossible not to have been struck with her appearance', but he was unable to dance with her as he had sprained his foot.

'I remember once to have sprained my ancle very violently many years ago', he wrote, 'and that the doctor ordered me to hold it under the pump two or three times a day. Now, in the United States of America, all is upon a grand scale, except taxation; and I am convinced that the traveller's ideas become much more enlarged as he journeys through the country. This being the case, I can easily account for the desire I felt to hold my sprained foot under the fall of Niagara. I descended the winding staircase which has been made for the accommodation of travellers, and then hobbled on to the scene of action. As I held my leg under the fall, I tried to meditate on the immense difference there was betwixt a house pump and this tremendous cascade of nature, and what effect it might have upon the sprain; but the magnitude of the subject was too overwhelming, and I was obliged to drop it.

'Perhaps, indeed, there was an unwarrantable tincture of vanity in an unknown wanderer wishing to have it in his power to tell the world, that he had held his sprained foot under a fall of water, which discharges six hundred and seventy thousand two hundred and fifty-five tons per minute. A gentle purling stream would have suited better ...'

The stairway to the foot of the north side of the American Falls had been built by Whitney in 1818. At the same time he had begun the operation of a ferry below the Falls in partnership with William Forsyth. Forsyth, who became the landlord of the Pavilion, the best known of the early hotels on the Canadian side, attempted to monopolize the tourist trade on that side of the river. However, the boundary line for private property fronting on the Canadian side of the river stopped one chain length (66 feet) short of the river bank; the actual frontage along the bank was reserved by the government and was known as the 'military reserve' or 'chain reserve'. When Forsyth attempted to fence in the reserve, he ran afoul of the lieutenant-governor, Sir Peregrine Maitland, who twice had the fences levelled by soldiers. Forsyth afterwards engaged in and lost a futile legal battle with the Crown, and finally in 1832 sold his property at Niagara to the promoters of 'The City of the Falls'—an unsuccessful attempt to establish a fashionable resort, which ended by exhibiting 'the deplorable aspect of three stuccoed cottages turned seedy, and a bare common, in place of a magnificent grove of chestnut trees'.

In 1825 the lease for the operation of the ferry on the Canadian side was given to Thomas Clark and Samuel Street, prominent local merchants and mill-owners, who were 'firmly bound and enjoined to carry across said ferry Indians and Soldiers with proper passports, or under the command of their officers without toll or reward'. They were also required to 'make construct and finish in a convenient, substantial and safe manner, a good and sufficient road, not less than Eighteen feet in width, with an easy and gradual descent ... down to the water's edge'. This road follows much the same course today as it did when it was built. Anthony Trollope commented after his first visit to America in 1861: 'The walk up the hill ... is very steep, and for those who have not good locomotive power of their own, will be found to be disagreeable ... In so short a distance I have always been ashamed to trust to other legs than my own, but I have observed that Americans are always dragged up. I have seen single young men of from eighteen to twenty-five, from whose outward appearance no story of idle, luxurious life can be read, carried about alone in carriages over distances which would be counted as nothing by any healthy English lady of fifty. None but the old invalids should require the assistance of carriages in seeing Niagara, but the trade in carriages is to all appearances the most brisk trade there.'

To the surprise of many visitors, the rowboats that ferried them across the river were perfectly safe, and not a single accident occurred before the ferry was discontinued with the completion of the Upper Suspension Bridge in 1869. Clark and Street did, however, receive a petition in 1842 complaining that 'the principle ferryman and his subordinate are both adicted to habits of intemperance ... that owing to their indulgence in strong drink they are often unaccommodating and uncivil to passengers – and as we are informed are in the habit of extorting from persons larger sums for ferriage than they are permited by their agreements with you to exact for their services'.

The Terrapin Tower, built on the brink of the Horseshoe Falls in 1833, was the first of many such structures at Niagara. Two wooden towers were built at Lundy's Lane to enable visitors to view the battlefield of 1814. '[American] tourists ... are very fond of visiting the battle-field, conceiving, I believe,' wrote W. H. G. Kingston, an English traveller, 'that they gained the victory, whereas the Britishers equally lay claim to the honour. The Irish car[riage]-drivers take ample advantage of this fancy, and drive the visitors about in all directions, with *naive* discursiveness narrating events which never occurred, and with equal talent selecting spots as remote from each other as possible for the scenes on which they pretend they took place.' The war was often a touchy subject. W. H. Smith wrote in his *Canadian Gazetteer* of 1846:

'A pamphlet is offered for sale here, called "Every Man his own Guide to the Falls of Niagara"; which, with a little information, contains a great deal of trash. It is the production of an American on the opposite side; and, while professing to point out all objects of interest about the Falls, it is evident the only object of the author, who keeps a shop on the American side, is to draw all travellers to that side, by painting everything to be seen there in the brightest colours, and throwing all points of interest on the Canadian side into the shade. One-and-twenty pages of this precious production are taken up with what the compiler calls a "chronological table, containing the principal events of the late war between the United States and Great Britain"; the whole of which might be summed up in four words – "*we licked the British*". To sell this pamphlet on the other side, in order to gratify the inordinate vanity of his countrymen, might answer the purpose of the author very well, and prove a profitable adjunct to his trade in walking sticks; but to send it over to Canada to be sold, is a piece of impudence almost unparalleled, even among the *free and independent citizens*.'

Navy Island became a tourist attraction after its brief occupation by the Patriots in the winter of 1837-38. According to Lieutenant Levinge, in *Echoes in the Backwoods*, 'walking-sticks, supposed to have been cut upon the island, are as eagerly bought by the visitors to the Falls of Niagara, as bullets and bits of iron are sought after by tourists on the plains of Waterloo; but, as the demand for the latter has far outrun the legitimate possibility of a supply, they are manufactured expressly. So the walking-sticks from Navy Island have been chiefly cut at the back of Mr. Starkey's shanty, at the Falls! – only four miles off, to be sure.'

'Daguerreotypes of the American fall are in great request,' wrote Charles Richard Weld, who visited Niagara in 1853, 'the proper thing according to Yankee notions, being for the purchaser to stand prominently in the foreground while the impression is taken'. John Werge, an English photographer who visited the Falls the following year, described how Platt D. Babbitt, 'a resident Daguerrean', had a pavilion at Prospect Point, 'under which his camera was in position all day long, and when a group of visitors stood on the shore to survey the Falls from that point, he took the group – without their knowledge – and showed it to the visitors before they left. In almost every instance he sold the picture at a good price; the people were generally delighted to be taken at the Falls'. Babbitt apparently gave up his little pavilion in the late fifties to run a store, opposite the Cataract House, where he had 'Indian-work, rock-work, fans, &c.' for sale, in addition to 'a large collection of views for the stereoscope'; his photographer's stand was taken over at first by James Thomson, and later by Samuel Mason. Among Babbitt's glass stereographs of Niagara is one of the Prince of Wales (later Edward VII) at Prospect Point on September 17, 1860.

'The first view which the Prince got of the cataract', Nicholas A. Woods, *The Times* special correspondent, reported, 'was on the evening of his arrival, when he saw them as no man had ever seen them before, and as they will probably never be seen again – he saw the Falls of Niagara illuminated! At the first idea it seems about as feasible to light up the Atlantic as those great outpourings of Lake Erie, and Mr. Blackwell, when he started the idea, was looked on as well meaning and all that, but chimerical, to use the mildest term. Mr. Blackwell, however, persevered, and had some 200 Bengal lights made of the very largest size which it was possible to manufacture. About 50 or 60 of these were placed in a row under the cliffs, beneath Clifton House, and facing the American Fall; 50 or 60 more were placed under Table Rock, and 50 or 60 behind the sheet of water itself ... At ten o'clock at night they were all lit, and their effect was something grand, magical, brilliant, and wonderful beyond all power of words to pourtray. In an instant the whole mass of water, glowing vivid, and as if incandescent in the intense light, seemed turned to molten silver. From behind the Fall the light shone with such dazzling brilliancy that the waters immediately before it looked like a sheet of crystal glass, a cascade of diamonds, every bead and stream in which leapt and sparkled and spread the glare over the whole scene, like a river of lighted phosphorus.'

On the following day the Prince saw Blondin 'execute his most terrific feat – that of crossing the Rapids on a tight rope with a man on his back'. After Blondin's performance, which included 'the still more dangerous task of returning along the rope *on stilts* about three feet high', the Prince made a sightseeing trip aboard the *Maid of the Mist*. This was the second boat of this name, and was a larger and more powerful steamer than the first which it replaced in 1854. The first *Maid of the Mist* had been launched in 1846 to ferry carriages across the river, but had had little success and, after the erection of Ellet's suspension bridge, had become a sightseeing boat.

The second *Maid of the Mist* was not as profitable as had been hoped, and in 1861 her owners had the opportunity to sell her on the Canadian side if she could be delivered at Lake Ontario. Joel R. Robinson agreed to pilot the boat through the rapids and whirlpool to the lower river with the assistance of the engineer and fireman. Much to the surprise of a large crowd which assembled to see the hair-raising trip, the steamer survived her buffeting in the rapids, and became 'the first boat that ever came to dock from up stream' at Queenston. According to Peter A. Porter, 'the collector of the port of Queenston at that time was a Scotchman, and not given to sentiment. He rushed down to the wharf and insisted that Robinson take out entrance and clearance papers. He did so, and the collector was not out his fees, though the manifest shows that the steamer carried "no passengers and no freight".' Twenty-five years later, sightseeing trips on the river immediately below the Falls were resumed by a third steamer named *Maid of the Mist.*

Many mid-nineteenth century visitors were appalled by the steadily increasing commercialization of the Falls. Thomas Rolph wrote after his visit in 1832 that only a few buildings could be seen 'peering from among the trees and shrubbery', but that he feared for the future. 'I wish', he wrote, 'it were provided by law that no building should be erected within sight of the little plot of ground immediately adjoining the cataract. As matters are now conducted, another twenty years may see the whole amphitheatre filled with grog-shops, humbug museums, &c., &c.' But only thirteen years later G. D. Warburton found Niagara 'overrun with every species of abominable fungus–the growth of rank bad taste: with equal luxuriance on the English and American sides, Chinese pagoda, menagerie, camera obscura, museum, watch-tower, wooden monument, tea gardens, "old curiosity shops" '. Warburton described how a boy handed him a slip of paper on which were printed what he sarcastically termed 'some stanzas of astounding magnificence':

'Would ye fain steal a glance o'er life's dark sea,
And gaze though trembling on eternity?
Would ye *look out, look down,* where God hath set
His mighty signet? Come–come higher yet,
To the PAGODA's utmost height ascend,
And see earth, air, and sky in one alembic blend!

'Pagoda is now open to visitors and perfectly secure ***
Admittance 25 cents *** 1st April, 1845.'

Even if the tourist felt that the 'puny efforts and bad taste of man' could do little to spoil the 'might and majesty' of Niagara, he could not avoid being pestered by guides, hackmen, pedlars, and touts for the hotels and sideshows. An act of the Legislative Assembly in 1853, 'to enable the Municipal Council of the Township of Stamford, to make By-Laws for the better government of that part of the said Township, which lies in the immediate vicinity of the Falls of Niagara', did nothing to improve the situation on the Canadian side, which was much the worst and a national disgrace.

The Table Rock House was particularly notorious. 'Upon arrival at the house,' the United States consul at Clifton reported in 1866, 'parties are immediately waited upon by some one of the employees, politely invited to enter the building, proceed to the observatory, below the rock, or "wherever they please", and in most cases assured that it is all "*quite free*" except what they choose to give to the guide, while the keeper of the house receives his pay in profits on such fancy articles as they desire to purchase. The [photographic] artist also solicits patronage, and offering to perform his work at low prices – which are four six or eight times less than afterwards collected – secures it.

'When the visitors are ready to depart they are reminded that they have bills to settle, and exorbitant prices are charged for use of oil cloth clothing, pictures, etc. In case of refusal to comply with these demands, the proprietors and employees of the house take the law into their own hands, the visitors are falsely imprisoned – not allowed to depart without paying every cent that it is thought fit to demand – insulted, assaulted and quite frequently knocked down, dragged out and otherwise maltreated.'

A Royal Commission report by E. B. Wood in 1873 admitted that 'the impositions have been carried on to such an extent and the difficulty of escape from the organized band of cabmen, fancy and variety store keepers, guides, sight showers, picture takers, oil clothes furnishers, conductors under what is alleged to be the sheet of water, hotel keepers and runners, all working to plunder ... has been so great as to elicit the comments of travellers and the criticisms of the public press throughout the civilized world.' Wood recommended that the Ontario government 'should itself assume the control and management of the chain reserve and of the descent to the foot of the Falls ... putting its own officers in charge', but no action was taken.

Tourists complained of the many charges for sightseeing, but the fee for admission to Prospect Park on the American side was defended in Faxon's *Illustrated handbook of travel* of 1874: 'No doubt the State of New York, years ago, ought to have reserved the lands lying along the Falls, as a part of the public domain, and made of them a free pleasure park; but the State did nothing of the kind. It sold grants of land to the settlers; and they have had to do the best they could. When Niagara first became a famous watering place, there were no improvements. Goat Island was almost inaccessible. There were no means of visiting the spots where now the most enjoyment is found. By degrees the islands have been opened to visitors, the ferry across the river established, the suspension bridges constructed. But Prospect Point – the projection of land directly abreast the American Falls, and from which one could toss a chip or even dip his hand into the very cataract – remained unimproved. It was a rough, rocky, scrubby cliff, covered with loose stones and gnarly trees, with no wall or railing even at the brink, to prevent the unwary from falling over; infested by peddlers, Indians, and vagabonds, and having no conveniences for the visitor. The land could not be made productive to the owners; for the hosts of visitors would constantly overrun it. So the owners associated themselves, and, at an expense of several thousand dollars, have enclosed the Point, built a solid and safe wall along the edge of the precipice and on the side towards the Fall, so that visitors, even children, can sit with perfect safety directly over the rushing torrent, and gaze into its foamy depths; built a safe and rapid inclined railway ... to the water's edge below the fall, built summer houses, cleared and beautified the grounds, supplied them with seats, &c. And because, for the enjoyment of all this, twenty-five cents admission is charged, a howl has gone up, forsooth, about "fencing in the Falls".'

At the opening of the state legislature in January 1879, Governor Lucius Robinson appealed for an end to the abuses at Niagara. He stated that 'it would seem to be incumbent' on the governments of New York State and the Province of Ontario to protect visitors from 'improper annoyance on either side', and told of a 'casual meeting and conversation' the previous summer with Lord Dufferin, then Governor-General of Canada, who had suggested to him that 'a sort of international park should be established, enclosing a suitable space on each side of the river from which all the annoyances and vexations ... should be excluded'. The matter was referred to the Commissioners of the State Survey, who appointed James T. Gardner, its director, and Frederick Law Olmsted, the famous landscape architect, to study the question. All recognized that the 'persecutions of hackmen, importunities of perambulating photographers, and all the pocket-draining exactions of endless gate-keepers and guides' were minor problems in relation to the need for the preservation of the scenery at the Falls.

The beauty of the American Rapids was ruined by a large paper mill on Bath Island, and on the opposite bank 'an unsightly rank of buildings in all stages of preservation and decay; small "hotels", mills, carpenter shops, stables, "bazaars", ice-houses, laundries with clothes hanging out to dry, bath houses, large, glaring white hotels, and an indescribable assortment of miscellaneous rookeries, fences, and patent medicine signs'. Only Goat Island was unspoiled; fortunately nothing had come of early proposals to exploit the island, such as General Porter's suggestion that it might be used as a state prison, but the future was uncertain to say the least.

'It is now a clearly recognized duty of governments', Gardner wrote in his report to the Commissioners, 'to reserve from sale parts of the public domain that contain natural features of such unusual character as to be objects of interest to the whole world, and whose perfection may be seriously marred by private ownership. Free enjoyment of these noblest works of nature is now felt to be one of man's most precious privileges, not to be abridged by private rights or greed for gain.'

Gardner stated that Congress had been 'acting on this principle' when it reserved the Yosemite Valley for public use in 1864, and designated Yellowstone as a National Park in 1872. He and Olmsted recommended that the paper mill on Bath Island and 'seven good buildings and ten of little value' on the main shore should be demolished, and a state reservation created along the river front from the head of the rapids to the Falls, including Prospect Park. Rowland F. Hill, whose profitable pulp mill was among the buildings scheduled for demolition, pointed out, not unreasonably, that there was no analogy to be made between Yosemite and Yellowstone, where the land was wilderness, and Niagara, where commercial development had taken place for nearly a century. Hill scoffed at the proposal to 'restore' the 'natural scenery' at the Falls – 'Whether it is also proposed to restore the primeval "fauna" or the "aborigines", does not appear', he wrote in an open letter to the state legislature.

A memorial in support of Lord Dufferin's suggestion of an international park was signed by nearly seven hundred of the leading men of Canada, Great Britain, and the United States; among these were Carlyle, Ruskin, Emerson, Longfellow, Parkman, Cyrus Field, Admiral David D. Porter, and General Nelson A. Miles. The petition, which was addressed to both the Governor of New York State and the Governor-General of Canada, undoubtedly impressed the supporters of the proposed reservation, but probably did little to dissuade its many opponents who regarded the scheme as 'one of the most unnecessary and unjustifiable raids upon the State Treasury ever attempted'. The latter were certainly not impressed by some remarkably snobbish propaganda which explained that Niagara was 'now given up to second-class tourists and excursionists who are brought by the car-load', that it was 'a rare thing to find any of the best people here', and that the excursion parties, who could be seen at Prospect Park 'fetching their own tea and coffee and provisions and enjoying a rollicking dance in the Pavilion', failed to derive the proper moral benefit from the Falls. J. B. Harrison, who wrote a series of letters in 1882 to various New York and Boston newspapers in support of the preservation of the Falls, had the good sense to defend the conduct of the much maligned excursionists: 'As to boisterous dancing, I can only say that I have each week attended the "hops" at the principal hotels, which are conducted by the guests, people of the highest social position and character, and have also looked on at all the dances in Prospect Park, and there were only very slight differences observable in the manners of the people at the different entertainments. Young people cannot sit in silence gazing at the Falls, through all of a long summer day, thinking of aesthetic sublimities, or communing with the Absolute and Infinite.'

It was not until 1883 that an act was passed by the New York State legislature 'to authorize the selection, location and appropriation of certain lands in the village of Niagara Falls for a state reservation; and to preserve the scenery of the falls of Niagara'. A board of five commissioners was appointed, and a tract of land, somewhat smaller than that recommended in 1879, was selected and appraised; it embraced 107 acres and was valued at almost a million and a half dollars. The bill for the appropriation was finally passed on April 30, 1885, after extensive lobbying by a number of prominent men, and on July 15 the State Reservation was officially opened with great fanfare and much oratory.

Thomas V. Welch, who had led the movement in the state legislature to 'free' Niagara, was appointed superintendent of the reservation. It was an immediate success. 'During the summer and autumn, as long as the pleasant weather continued,' Welch wrote in his first report, 'a constant stream of people visited Niagara, ranging in number from 1,000 to 6,000 daily, at least four times as many as before the establishment of the reservation. Fears were entertained that the freedom extended to all comers would result in license, in the destruction of property and the loss of life from accident. Such fears proved to be groundless, a sense of personal interest and ownership seemed to impress itself upon all, and to make each visitor in a manner custodian of the place. Great crowds came and went as quietly and orderly as if the reservation had been established for years ... One of the most noticeable results immediately following the establishment of the reservation, was the increased number of visitors apparently of limited means. Many of these people lived within a short distance of Niagara, but had been deterred from seeing it by the fees heretofore charged for admission to the grounds.' Welch ended his report with the note that 'It is probable that in the near future the complete preservation of the scenery of the falls of Niagara will be assured by the establishment of a reservation on the Canadian shore'.

The original plans of Gardner and Olmsted included both sides of the river, although, of course, they had 'more particular reference to the American side'. At a conference held in September 1879 between the Commissioners of the State Survey and members of the Ontario government, the Canadian representatives 'expressed their entire sympathy with the project,' but pointed out that since the chain reserve along the river front was the property of the federal government, 'it was only reasonable that the cost of restoring the scenery should fall upon the Dominion Government, which ... was, therefore, in a much better position than the Province to take up the work'. However, it soon became obvious that the federal government had not the slightest intention of establishing a Canadian park, which it felt would set a precedent and open a door for similar demands from other provinces. On March 30, 1885, three and a half months before the opening of the State Reservation, the Ontario government passed an act 'for the preservation of the natural scenery about Niagara Falls'. Two years later 'The Queen Victoria Niagara Falls Park Act' established the park which was opened to the public on May 24, 1888.

Gardner and Olmsted had planned to restore the natural scenery, and not merely create public parks at the Falls. At the time they made their report, the communities on both sides of the river were little more than villages, and they could not foresee the vast impact of the power development that took place at Niagara at the end of the nineteenth century, to say nothing of that of the automobile in the twentieth century. Restoration was a dream, but their report led to the establishment of governmental control which has done much to protect Niagara from the assaults of our industrial society.

A

Handbill of Samuel Hooker, 1821
Buffalo & Erie County Historical Society
Bath Island, now known as Green Island, was given its name because of the bath house built there by Hooker, who was the first man to make a living as a guide at the Falls.

B

The Clifton House
Pencil sketch by J. R. Coke Smyth, 1838
Royal Ontario Museum

C

The Clifton House – hotel bill, 1864
The Clifton House, built in 1833, had a superb location, overlooking both the American and Horseshoe Falls, at the head of the road leading down to the ferry. It was considerably enlarged in later years, when it became the most famous hotel on the Canadian side and the favourite resort of English visitors. The Clifton House suffered the fate of almost all the nineteenth-century hotels at Niagara when it was destroyed by fire in 1898.

D

The Cataract House – advertising card, *c.* 1865

E

The Cataract House and the International Hotel
From a stereograph by Platt D. Babbitt
The International Hotel, which was built in 1853
on the site of the Eagle Tavern,
rivalled the nearby Cataract House.
Both hotels overlooked the American Rapids,
and had 'river parlours' –
huge wings that extended to the river bank –
which were 'splendidly furnished, the most exquisite taste and
the most costly fabrics and workmanship being displayed'.

F

The ferry landing, Canadian side
From a stereograph published by E. Anthony
c. 1860

G

Termination Rock certificate, 1835

H

Below Table Rock
From a stereograph, *c.* 1870
Stairways were built at Table Rock to the foot of the gorge,
where visitors dressed in oilcloths
were led by a guide under
the 'Great Falling Sheet of Water'
to Termination Rock.
The Cave of the Winds was a similar attraction
on the Goat Island side
of the American Falls.

I

Daguerreotype
Probably by Platt D. Babbitt, *c.* 1855

J

Ambrotype, *c.* 1857
The most popular spot for photographers
on the Canadian side
was immediately opposite the American Falls,
which thereby served as a background for their customers.
It was not until the later years of the nineteenth century
that visitors were photographed in a studio
with a painted background of the Falls.

K

The Clifton Depot, Great Western Railway
Stereograph by William England, 1859
The best-known early photographs of Niagara
were the series of stereographs taken by William England
for the London Stereoscopic Company in 1859.
Fortunately England photographed not only the Falls
but much of the contemporary scene at Niagara,
such as the Clifton Depot
at the Canadian end of Roebling's suspension bridge
which can be seen in the background.

L

Advertisement on the back of a photograph
by Samuel Mason, *c.* 1865

M

The Prince of Wales at Prospect Point
17 September 1860
From a stereograph by Platt D. Babbitt

N

Russian naval officers at Prospect Point
October, 1863
From a stereograph by Platt D. Babbitt
In 1863, the Czar, who was afraid of
possible intervention by the European powers
during his suppression of the Polish rebellion,
ordered the best ships of the Russian Atlantic and Pacific squadrons
to New York and San Francisco,
to prevent these ships being ice-bound in their own harbours
in the event of war.
The arrival of these ships in the middle of the Civil War
was wrongly interpreted
as a friendly gesture towards the Union cause,
and their officers were royally entertained.
Officers from five ships at New York
made a special trip to see Niagara.

O

Advertisement for Barnett's Museum
in *Smith's Canadian Gazetteer*, 1846
The museum of Thomas Barnett was praised by most visitors,
who generally censured the 'frippery curiosity-shops'
which lined the Canadian bank.
A 'Wild West' buffalo hunt staged by Barnett in 1872
was a fiasco, and a financial disaster
which led to the sale of the museum, five years later,
to his unscrupulous competitor, Saul Davis of the Table Rock House.

P

The second *Maid of the Mist*
From a stereograph by William England, 1859
Collection of Lura Woodside Watkins

Q

Interior of the 'Shadow of the Rock' dressing-rooms
From a stereograph by George Barker
c. 1875

R

Incline Railway and 'Shadow of the Rock' dressing-rooms
at the foot of the American Falls
From a stereograph, *c.* 1870

S

Interior of the Incline Railway
From a stereograph by George E. Curtis, *c.* 1870
The Incline Railway, operated by water power,
was built in 1845 to replace the stairway
to the ferry landing on the American side.
It was here that the 'Shadow of the Rock'
was introduced in the late sixties
as a rival attraction to the Cave of the Winds.
The former was demolished shortly after
its acquisition by the State Reservation.

T

Indian store and toll-gate on Bath Island
From a stereograph by John P. Heywood, *c.* 1865

U

Indian women selling bead-work on Goat Island
From a stereograph by George Barker, *c.* 1870

V

Invitation to the opening of the State Reservation
15 July 1885

W

Tugby's Bazaar

Photograph, *c.* 1880

Niagara Mohawk Power Corporation

Tugby's Mammoth Bazaar
had 'a full and complete collection of curiosities,
articles representative of Indian life and manners,
toys, bijouterie, fancy goods, and all similar products'.
It was the largest of the many stores
catering to the tourists, and was one of the buildings
removed after the establishment of
the State Reservation.

X

'Along the line of the Niagara Falls Park & River Ry.'

Panoramic guide, *c. 1895*

The Commissioners of the Queen Victoria Park
were disturbed by the fact that many of the excursionists
'crossing Lake Ontario by steamer from Toronto,
or elsewhere, found it much more convenient
to take the observation trains
of the New York Central Railway, at Lewiston,
which afforded partial views of the lower reach of the gorge,
and landed the excursionists
within a few minutes' walk
of the Park and river on the American side'.
It was then decided
to build the first electric railway at Niagara,
the Niagara Falls Park & River Railway,
which was opened in 1893
and provided an easy attractive route
along the Canadian side of the Niagara River
from Queenston to Chippawa.
Two years later the Niagara Gorge Railroad was opened
on the American side.
The two railways eventually merged and were connected by bridges
at Queenston–Lewiston and Niagara Falls.
'The Great Gorge Route' survived a number of fatal accidents,
but finally was closed down in 1935
after a landslide destroyed a large part of the track.

Y

Ice-bridge

From a stereograph by George Barker, *c.* 1890

The ice-bridges were a bonanza to the hotel proprietors,
bazaar men, and guides, who could not normally
expect much business in winter.
Shanties were erected on the ice and liquor was sold illegally.
When arrests were made, the boundary line
was invariably disputed at the trial –
if this was in Canada, the defendant claimed that his shanty
was in the United States, and *vice versa*.
Since the ice-bridge disintegrated after a few days,
the defendants usually avoided conviction.
It became illegal to cross the ice after 1912,
when a sudden break-up trapped three tourists
who lost their lives.

Bath Island,

NIAGARA FALLS.

THE Subscriber has erected, on this Island, an establishment for the accommodation of Ladies and Gentlemen visiting the Falls, consisting of a building, containing

WARM, COLD and SHOWERING BATHS,

Situated in a beautiful and retired spot, and supplied with the pure and limpid waters of Lake Erie, unadulterated by the streams that fall into the river between the Lake and the Falls, and often discolor the water along the main shores—Also a building situated in á different part of the Island, where he keeps a choice assortment of Liquors and other refreshments; and several Rooms where Gentlemen may find agreeable and healthful amusements.

BATH ISLAND contains about one acre and a half of ground, and is covered with forest trees, amongst which are several clusters of evergreens, where the subscriber is forming tasteful and romantic arbors and walks. Surrounded by the cool and crystal waters of the Lakes; fanned, during the summer months, by a mild and constant current of pure air produced by the motion of the waters; refreshed by the shades of cedars, maples, linn, and poplars; and undisturbed by the intrusions of a single insect, this spot possesses, in an eminent degree, the combined advantages of healthfulness and comfort, and as regards scenery, the most vivid fancy can depict nothing more beautifully wild and romantic than that which is here presented. Situated in the great Rapids of the Niagara, only one hundred yards above the Falls, and mid way between Goat or Iris Island and the American shore, and surrounded by groupes of smaller Islands on which the foot of man has never trod, the imagination may feast itself, for days and weeks, on its variegated wonders and beauties without fatigue.

It has, until very recently, been customary for strangers to visit the Falls on the British, rather than on the American side of the river, on account of the badness of the roads and want of comfortable Inns on the latter. These roads however, which three years ago were nearly impassable for carriages, have of late been materially improved, and are now as good as almost any roads in the country: And the spacious HOTEL lately erected by *P. Whitney*, Esq. and which is only two hundred yards from the subscriber's establishment, furnishes, it is believed, as good accommodations as any public house in the vicinity of the Falls, on either side. Independent of these considerations, the Bridge and road from the American shore to Iris Island and which passes across Bath Island; the enclosed stair-way for descending the Bank; and the Ferry below the Falls, afford an opportunity to visitors of examining this stupendous work of nature in all its various and interesting points of view, and give a decided preference to the American, over the British side.

The subscriber will use every exertion to contribute, in his department, to the comfort and satisfaction of the public, and confidently hopes that his endeavors to please will meet with correspondent patronage.

Niagara, July 3d, 1821. **SAMUEL HOOKER.**

SALISBURY'S PRINT—Buffalo.

B

CLIFTON HOUSE

NIAGARA FALLS—CANADA SIDE.

JOSLIN & DUNKLEE, Proprietors.

Visitors arriving by Railway, should have their baggage checked for, and stop at Suspension Bridge, where Omnibusses and Porters will be in attendance. Fare to House including Bridge Tolls & Baggage 25 cents.

1 Augt 1864

Mr. Wm H Scrugham Dr.

Bar 50 Cage 1.	1.50
Omnibus to House	~~50~~
Board 2 persons 2 days	16 00
Omnibus & Bridge Ticket	50
	$18.~~50~~

Paid

C

CATARACT HOUSE
NIAGARA FALLS.
WHITNEY, JERAULD & CO.
PROPRIETORS.
The Sage, Sons & Co. Lith. Prt'g & Mf'g Co. Buffalo, New York.
(Over.)

CATARACT HOUSE
REAR VIEW.
CATARACT HOUSE
WHITNEY, JERAULD & CO.
PROPRIETORS.
The Sage, Sons & Co. Lith. Prt'g & Mf'g Co. Buffalo, New York.
(Over.)

D

E

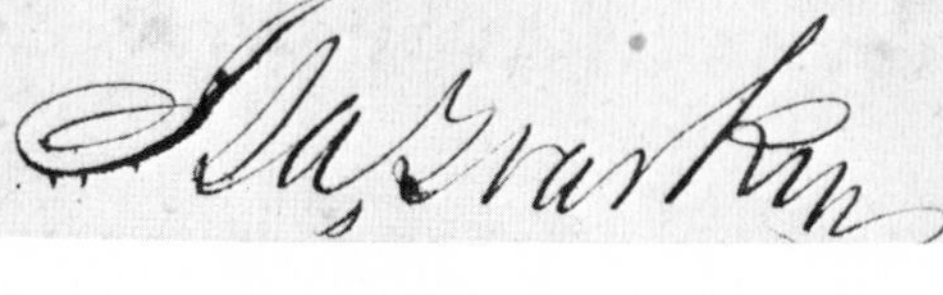

THIS MAY CERTIFY, THAT

Mr Harmon Noble

Has passed behind the Great Falling Sheet of Water to

"TERMINATION ROCK."

Given under my hand, at the Office of the General Register of the Names of Visitors, at the Table Rock, this 14th day of Augst 1835

F G

H

I

J

No. 197.—Clifton Depot or Station, Great Western Railway, Canada

K

M

N

P

DRESS and GUIDE
ONE DOLLAR

SHADOW OF THE ROCK
DRESSING ROOMS
FOR
LADIES & GENTLEMEN

Q R

S

DEAN'S METAMORA
INDIAN DEPOT
COMMUTATION FOR CROSSING
FOR THE SEASON ONE DOLLAR
25 Cts For CROSSING And RECROSSING
THIS BRIDGE PAYABLE HERE.
SODA
WATER

T

U

COMMISSIONERS:
William Dorsheimer,
Andrew H. Green,
Martin B. Anderson,
J. Hampden Robb,
Sherman S. Rogers.

Lucius Robinson 1879.
Grover Cleveland 1883.
David B. Hill 1885.

Lord Dufferin 1879.

THE CITIZENS OF NIAGARA FALLS

request the honor of your presence at the Opening of the State Reservation at Niagara

Wednesday, July 15th 1885, at noon.

The Commissioners of the State Reservation will in behalf of the State of New York take possession of the lands selected for the preservation of the scenery of the Falls of Niagara.

RECEPTION COMMITTEE:
F. Spalding, S. Geyer, F. R. Delano, A. Schoellkopf, Hans Nielson, S. M. N. Whitney, T. V. Welch, Benj. Rhodes, O. W. Cutler.

C. B. Gaskill, President.
A. H. Gluck, Secretary.
F. R. Delano, Treasurer.

INVITATION COMMITTEE:
F. R. Delano, Hans Nielson, William Pool, T. V. Welch, S. M. N. Whitney, G. M. Colburn, Benj. Flagler.

W

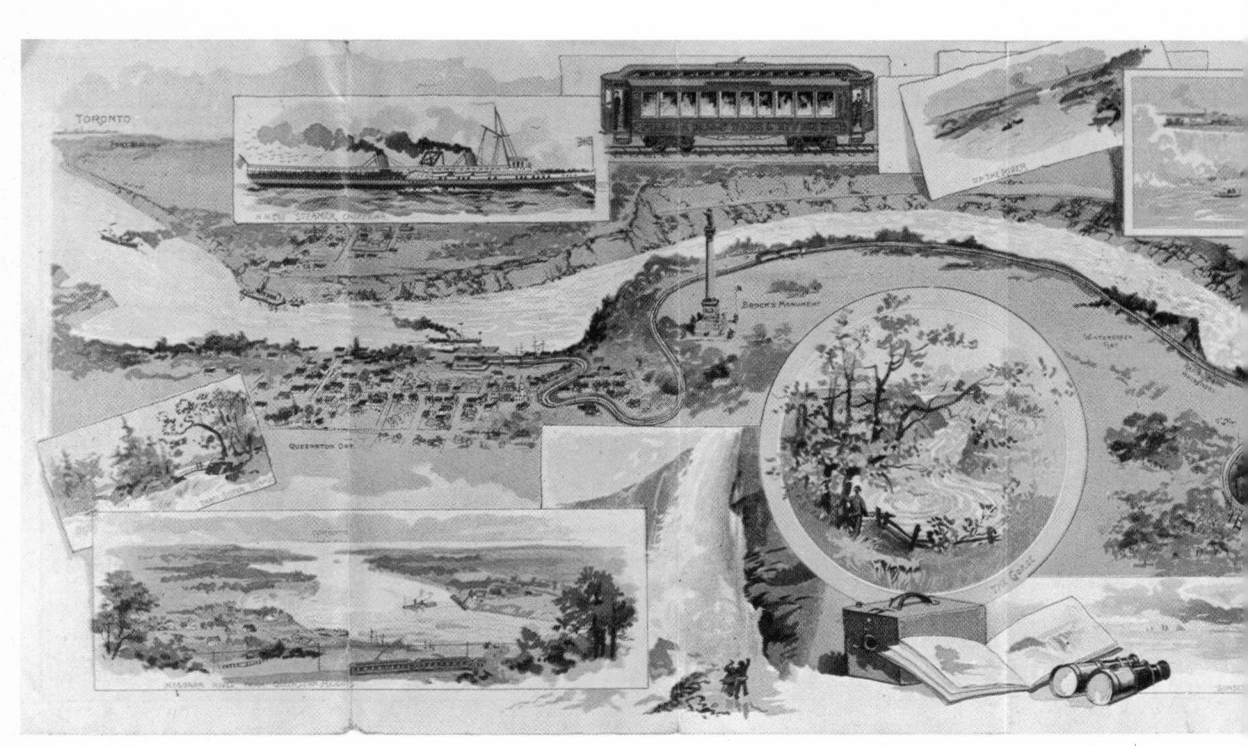
TORONTO
QUEENSTON ONT.
BROCK'S MONUMENT
UP THE RIVER
WINTERGREEN FLAT
THE GORGE

BUFFALO, N.Y.
NIAGARA ON THE LAKE
DUFFERIN ISLANDS
ALONG THE LINE OF THE
RA FALLS PARK & RIVER RY.

Y

POWER

'O what a waste of water-power is here! 'Twould move ten thousand water-wheels and run them thro' the year!' wrote an early nineteenth-century visitor to the Falls. Another visitor, Auguste Levasseur, noted that here was 'an incalculable moving power for machinery'. Levasseur was secretary to Lafayette, and he and the general were the guests of Judge Augustus Porter during their stay at Niagara in 1825. 'I do not think', wrote Levasseur, 'that Mr. Porter will long delay to take advantage of the benefits presented by such a spot.' That same year Judge Porter and his brother, General Peter B. Porter, 'proprietors of the lands which embrace the Rapids and Falls, on the American side of the Niagara', made the first significant attempt to develop the potential hydraulic power at the Falls.

A few months before the opening of the Erie Canal on October 26, 1825, virtually ended their lucrative portage business, the Porters issued an 'Invitation to Eastern Capitalists & Manufacturers' to develop 'hydraulic operations' on the upper rapids. 'Practically speaking', they declared, 'the extent to which water power may be here applied is without limit.' They drew attention to the fact that 'A number of manufactories, on a scale adapted to the wants of the immediate vicinity, have already been erected, and are now in successful operation at this place; among which are, a large and valuable grist mill, saw mill, two woollen cloth factories, two clothier's shops, several carding and spinning machines, a forge, paper mill, &c.' The Porters had hopefully named the original settlement Manchester – 'What a romantic name and what associations!' an English visitor commented sarcastically. However, little or no interest was shown in their proposed large-scale development.

In January 1847 Judge Porter, whose brother had died some three years before, issued a new circular addressed 'To Capitalists and Manufacturers'. He offered 'to sell the right of constructing and using' a proposed 'hydraulic canal' approximately three-quarters of a mile long, to be built diagonally from the river above the rapids to the gorge about half a mile below the Falls. The canal was to terminate in a reservoir along the high bank of the lower river, where mills were to be located. The circular included a map by Peter Emslie, a civil engineer, who estimated 'the whole cost of the canal, with its appurtenances, of sufficient capacity to afford water power for at least sixty run of mill stone, within the sum of Thirty thousand dollars'.

In 1849, before there was any response to his proposal, Augustus Porter died. But his second prospectus had created an interest in the project; the land needed for the canal and terminal basin was acquired from the Porter heirs by the Niagara Falls Hydraulic Company, incorporated on March 19, 1853. When this company attempted to blast through the solid Niagara limestone with gunpowder, the only explosive available at the time, it soon found that the costs of construction were formidable, and the work of excavation had to be suspended after little more than a year. Additional capital was acquired, and the company reorganized as the Niagara Falls Water Power Company in 1856. Work began again. Again the company exhausted its capital, and when it was unable to raise further money, the property was sold in 1860. Yet a third company, the Niagara Falls Canal Company, attempted to complete the project after the Civil War, when the work of excavation was made easier by the use of dynamite.

In 1875, the flour mill of Charles B. Gaskill was built on the canal basin on the high bank of the gorge. The mill was equipped with a wooden wheel that operated under a 25-foot head; after the water passed the wheel, it escaped through a short tail-race tunnel and was discharged from the face of the cliff into the gorge nearly two hundred feet below – less than one-eighth of the available head was used. This was the first and only use made of the canal before the creditors of the Canal Company foreclosed. On May 1, 1877, the company's entire property, on which more than $800,000 had been spent since 1853, was sold by auction to Jacob F. Schoellkopf, a Buffalo manufacturer, for $71,000. The following year, a new company was incorporated by Schoellkopf under the name of The Niagara Falls Hydraulic Power and Manufacturing Company. The canal was improved and enlarged, and by 1882 the 'hydraulic company' was supplying water power to seven mills located on the canal basin.

Electricity was to become the key to the development of Niagara power. Scant notice was paid, however, to the pioneer demonstration of hydro-electric power at the Falls. This took place on July 2, 1879, when 'the Brush Electric Light apparatus in Prospect Park became so far completed that the machine was put in motion for the first time' – the generator was run by a Lessner turbine wheel. The introduction of arc lights was given only a short paragraph in the *Niagara Falls Gazette* a week later. 'The electric light apparatus seems to be all that its inventor claims for it', the newspaper reported, 'and the lamps certainly yield a most beautiful and powerful light.' Almost as much space was devoted to the lawn party and concert of the ladies of St. Peter's Episcopal Church, which took place in Prospect Park the same evening. The 'Electric Light' became merely one of the park's many attractions, all of which were intended 'to amuse and instruct those who might otherwise become weary of the scene, and fail to appreciate it'.

In November 1881 the Brush Electric Light and Power Company of Niagara was organized. This company, headed by Arthur Schoellkopf, son of Jacob Schoellkopf and the active manager of the hydraulic company, installed an arc light machine in Quigley's Mill on the canal basin. The direct-current brush dynamo was similar to the one in Prospect Park, and was capable of supplying sixteen 2,000 candle-power open arc lamps. These were installed in two mills, several stores, an office building, and the *Gazette* office. This was the first public distribution of electricity at Niagara.

An entirely new scheme for the harnessing of Niagara power was suggested by Thomas Evershed, a divisional engineer of the Erie Canal, in a letter published by the *Lockport Union*, February 3, 1886:

'Beginning at a point in the gorge below Niagara Falls just north of the state reservation and upper Suspension Bridge, and about twelve feet above the surface of the water, run a tunnel so as to strike the river above the mouth of the hydraulic canal, a distance of about five thousand feet, then continue the tunnel under the river's edge, say, five thousand six hundred feet farther, making two miles of tunnel.

'This last mentioned 5600 feet can be utilized as a tail-race for factories taking water from the river close by.

'With wheel-pits sunk in the rock this water could be used with turbine wheels under a head of eighty to one hundred feet... A hole or holes drilled from the bottom of these wheel-pits into the tunnel below, will take off the water so used.

'The wheels could be placed every twenty-five feet apart if necessary, and the power cabled off to any point desired, running any number of mills and factories of any size from the making of toothpicks to a Krupp's foundry.'

Evershed's letter immediately attracted the attention of several local manufacturers, and The Niagara River Hydraulic Tunnel, Power and Sewer Company was organized with Charles B. Gaskill as president and Evershed as engineer. The letter had made no mention of the use of water power to produce electricity, but the new company's prospectus of August 1886 emphasized the potential importance of hydro-electric power: 'It is conceded by leading practical electricians that it would be entirely practicable now to light the city of Buffalo (distance 20 miles) with power furnished by Niagara Falls, and the opinion is rife among scientific men that ways will be found in the near future for transmitting this power to much greater distances and for using it in many new ways. Should this be done, the unlocking of this great natural store-house of power, which is proposed in this prospectus, will bear an importance not exceeded by any private or public work in the State.' The very magnitude of the project defeated the local promoters of the tunnel company in their attempts to finance it, and, after the name of the company had been changed to The Niagara Falls Power Company, the ownership was acquired by The Cataract Construction Company, a syndicate which included J. P. Morgan, William K. Vanderbilt, and most of the other leading New York financiers.

It was estimated that the proposed tunnel, 2½ miles long and 14 feet in diameter, would be adequate for the discharge from 238 mills, each supplied with power by its own 500 horse-power water-wheel. The total output – 119,000 horse-power – exceeded the 'combined available power in use' at half-a-dozen leading manufacturing towns. 'How and where the proposed enormous amount of power could be so used as to justify the undertaking financially' was the major question facing the Cataract Company. It was obvious that Niagara Falls, N.Y., with a population of less than five thousand, could consume only a fraction of this power. Buffalo, with a quarter of a million population, presented an immediate market, but was twenty miles away. A thorough investigation of Evershed's scheme not only revealed that the mill-over-the-wheel-pit plan would involve prohibitive construction costs, but led to the radical decision to develop power at one central station and distribute it by some means of transmission, probably electricity, to the places where it could be used.

No hydraulic power development of comparable size had ever been built, and electrical power transmission was still at a pioneer stage. At the suggestion of the president of the Cataract Construction Company, Edward Dean Adams, the International Niagara Commission was organized in London in June 1890 'to ascertain the best system for the Niagara enterprise in the opinion of the highest available scientific authorities'. Sir William Thomson (later Lord Kelvin) presided over the Commission, the other members of which were Dr. Coleman Sellers of Philadelphia, the company's chief engineer, Professor E. Mascart of Paris, Colonel Theodore Turrettini of Geneva, and Professor W. C. Unwin of London, who acted as secretary. A competition was held. A number of engineers in England, France, Germany, Hungary, Switzerland, and the United States were invited 'to submit projects for the development, transmission and distribution of about 125,000 effective horse-power on the shafts of water motors at the Falls of Niagara'.

Fourteen projects, which included various schemes for transmission by electricity, compressed air, and wire ropes, were considered by the Commission in early 1891, but none of the plans submitted 'could be recommended for adoption without considerable modification'. The highest prize, $500, was awarded to the joint submission of Faesch & Piccard and Cuénod, Sautter & Company, both of Geneva, for a project combining hydraulic development and electrical distribution of power. (Faesch & Piccard were to make the complete working drawings for the 5,000 horse-power turbines that were eventually installed in Power-House Number One.) Unwin reported that 'the general opinion of the Commission was in favor of the adoption of electrical methods as the chief means of distributing the power, though perhaps not as the only means'. Two of the competitors, Ganz & Company of Budapest, and Professor George Forbes of London, had proposed the use of alternating current generators, but the Commission was 'not convinced of the advisability of departing from the older and better understood methods of continuous currents'. The advantages of alternating current were only beginning to be explored, and many experts, including Sir William Thomson, were curiously opposed to it. Thomson, in fact, had attempted to exclude the consideration of alternating current systems by the Commission, but had been prevented from doing so by Coleman Sellers.

In the United States, George Westinghouse, the inventor of the air brake, had become interested in the development of alternating current some years earlier. In 1885 he had acquired the rights to the Gaulard-Gibbs transformer, which had solved the problem of power losses in electrical transmission. (Power losses are directly proportional to the square of the current, hence a ten-fold reduction in current produces a hundred-fold reduction in power losses. The A.C. transformer stepped up the voltage and thereby reduced the current for economical transmission; the high-tension power transmitted was then stepped down by a similar transformer for distribution at a convenient lower voltage.) In 1886 the Westinghouse Electric Company installed the first commercial A.C. lighting plant at Buffalo, and so started the 'great power fight' with the Edison Electric Company. Thomas A. Edison had designed a complete D.C. incandescent lighting system and had successfully demonstrated it on a large scale in 1882, when his Pearl Street generating station was opened in New York. The low constant-voltage system of Edison was much superior to and safer for indoor use than the earlier arc lighting systems, but it had a serious limitation in the short distance to which current could be transmitted economically. Faced with the competition of alternating current, the Edison Electric Company bitterly opposed its use and widely publicized the latent danger in high voltage transmission. In 1888 Westinghouse obtained the patents issued to Nikola Tesla for his induction motor and polyphase system of alternating current, which eventually were to become indispensable to the large-scale industrial use of electrical power. Westinghouse, however, had refused to enter the competition of the International Niagara Commission. He told one of his engineers that 'these people are trying to get $100,000 worth of information for a prize of $3,000. When they are ready to do business, we will submit a plan and bid for the work'.

The only important feature of the Evershed plan that was finally adopted was the enormous discharge tunnel to be built under the village of Niagara Falls. But its design was considerably changed – its length was reduced to 6,700 feet, and a horseshoe form used instead of the circular tunnel proposed by Evershed. Work on this tunnel began on October 4, 1890, more than a year before the Cataract Construction Company formally decided to establish 'a central station for the generation and distribution of electrical energy for lighting and power purposes'. On December 14, 1891, letters inviting tenders for electrical equipment were sent to six American and Swiss firms, including the Westinghouse Company. 'After protracted and exhaustive examination of many plans', the Niagara Falls Power Company finally signed a contract with Westinghouse on October 27, 1893, for 'the construction and installation of three alternating-current dynamos of 5000 horse-power each', five times larger than any previously built. The system adopted involved 'the use of two-phase current with a frequency of 25 periods per second generated at a voltage of 2000 and the use of transformers for long-distance transmission at a higher tension'.

Commercial operations began in August 1895. The first two generating units were put into service, and power was supplied to the Pittsburgh Reduction Company (later the Aluminum Company of America). This was the first use of Niagara power by the electro-chemical industry. Niagara became a magnet for the newly developing industry, which needed a source of low-cost, continuous, electrical power for its electrolytic and electrothermic processes. A transmission line was built to Buffalo in 1896, and current was turned on the line on November 15 of the same year. By 1900 all ten generating units in Power-House Number One were in service, and work had already begun on Power-House Number Two. These two power-houses became known in 1927 as the Adams Station. The Westinghouse generators in Power-House Number One remained in use for more than half a century until the Adams generating plant was closed down on September 30, 1961, when the first of the units was given to the Smithsonian Institution.

The success of the world's first major hydro-electric plant was demonstrated at the Pan-American Exposition at Buffalo in 1901, when the exhibition was lighted by electricity generated at the Falls. A great expansion of the pioneer development soon followed. Three generating stations were built on the Canadian side of the river. By 1910 the total capacity of all these developments was approximately 400,000 horse-power, of which about half was generated on the Canadian side. Electricity has transformed society, and the story of electric power in the twentieth century is one of immense expansion and technical development. This expansion and development was based on the successful 'harnessing' of Niagara.

A

'Invitation to Eastern Capitalists & Manufacturers'
Broadsheet, 1825
Buffalo & Erie County Historical Society

B

Augustus Porter
Lithograph, from a daguerreotype, in Orsamus Turner's
Pioneer history of the Holland Purchase of Western New York
1849

C

Wood-engraving by J. W. Orr
for label of Porter's Mills, *c.* 1840
In 1826 Albert H. Porter, son of Augustus Porter,
entered into partnership with H. W. Clarke, who had
started to manufacture paper at his mill on Bath Island
in the fall of 1825.
The business was sold in 1848, and
eventually became known as
the Niagara Falls Paper Manufacturing Company.
By the eighties the company's mills on Bath Island
covered more than three acres
and were producing 12,000 lbs per day.
These mills were razed after
the establishment of the State Reservation in 1885,
when a new mill was built on the hydraulic canal.

D

Map by Peter Emslie
of the proposed hydraulic canal, 1846

E

Mills on the 'high bank'
served by the hydraulic canal, 1895
Niagara Mohawk Power Corporation
The mills remained an eyesore at Niagara for many years. It was not until after World War II that the industrial complex on the high bank was finally demolished to create part of a scenic highway from the Falls to Fort Niagara. The last use of the water from the hydraulic canal ceased when the Schoellkopf Power Station at a foot of the gorge was partially destroyed by a rock-slide in June 1956.

F

Installation of the second penstock
of the Hydraulic Station Number Two, 1898
Niagara Mohawk Power Corporation
In 1895-96 the 'hydraulic company', which had its first generating station in Quigley's Mill, built a second power station in the gorge at the water's edge. This station, which used the full effective drop of 210 feet between the head of the rapids and the Maid-of-the-Mist pool below the Falls, was so successful that it was immediately enlarged. The 11-foot penstock built from the forebay at the top of the cliff to the power-house below was the largest in the world at the time. About 90 per cent of the output of the station was direct current supplied to the nearby industries, the largest of which was the Pittsburgh Reduction Company (later the Aluminum Company of America). The steel arch bridge designed by L. L. and R. S. Buck can be seen nearing completion in this photograph. The bridge, consisting of a pair of parallel arched trusses with a span of 840 feet, was the largest of its kind to be built in the nineteenth century. This famous bridge, known as the Falls View Bridge, replaced the second Upper Suspension Bridge built in 1889 (the first bridge fell into the river during a storm on the night of January 10 of that year). On January 27, 1938, an ice jam in the gorge sheared the arch at its hinges and the steel bridge collapsed on to the ice.

G

Plan for turbine installation
submitted to the International Niagara Commission
by Faesch & Piccard, 1890
Smithsonian Institution

H

Construction shaft for the discharge tunnel, *c*. 1891
Niagara Mohawk Power Corporation

I

The wheel-pit extension under construction, December 1897
Niagara Mohawk Power Corporation
The successful operation of the first hydro-electric units in Power-House Number One led to the extension of the generating station and wheel-pit slot to provide for ten complete units. The wheel-pit was 20 feet wide and 178 feet deep; steel penstocks 7 feet 6 inches in diameter delivered water under a 135-foot head to the turbines installed at the bottom of the pit.

J

Installation of a Westinghouse generator
in Power-House Number One, *c*. 1898
Niagara Mohawk Power Corporation

K

A repair wagon and the first Buffalo transmission line
Niagara Mohawk Power Corporation

L

Pan-American Exposition poster
Colour lithograph by Evelyn Rumsey Cary

Niagara Falls.

Invitation to Eastern Capitalists & Manufacturers.

THE subscribers are proprietors of the lands which embrace the Rapids and Falls, on the American side, of the Niagara; and also of *Iris*, *Bath*, and the other small islands lying in the rapids, and connected, by bridges, with the main shore. This situation is not surpassed, and probably not equalled, in the United States, as a site for the establishment of manufactures, whether viewed in reference to its intrinsic advantages, or to its exterior facilities for the collection of manufacturing materials, and the distribution of fabrics. The country in the vicinity of the Falls is rich in soil, romantically beautiful in formation, and proverbial for salubrity. The pure and limpid waters of the Niagara—always flowing with an uniform current, and full banks—are as propitious to the health, as they are condusive to the comfort and luxury of its inhabitants. From the head of the rapids to the great Falls, a distance of three fourths of a mile, there is a regular succession of *chutes*, which give, in the aggregate, sixty feet of perpendicular descent; and the adjoining banks appear to have been expressly designed for the convenience of leading water from the river for hydraulic operations. Practically speaking, the extent to which water power may be here applied is whithout limit. A thousand mills might be erected with the same ease, and equally accessible, as if on a plain; and each supplied with a never failing water power, at an expence not exceeding fifty dollars, and be at the same time, perfectly secure against the dangers of inundation. This position is connected with the grand canal by an excellent boat navigation of ten miles in length, terminating in the canal at the mouth of Tonnewanta creek, through a lock of five feet lift—and with Erie and the other western Lakes, by a safe and uninterrupted sloop navigation. In the opposite direction, it is only seven miles distant from Lewiston, the head of the sloop navigation of Lake Ontario & the St. Lawrence. The communication with Lewiston is, at present, by a good road, but will probably soon be improved by the substitution of a canal or railway. The extensive forests which border the Niagara, the lake and the canal, and cover the islands in the river, will furnish a cheap and abundant supply of fuel for manufacturing purposes, for many years to come; and until the canals, already commenced, between Lake Erie and the Ohio, shall open a ready and cheap access to the vast beds of stone coal with which the whole of that region abounds. Adjoining and attached to the mill seats, the subscribers own a tract of land on the main shore, amply sufficient for the site of a large town, which must soon grow up at this place; and for the accommodation of its inhabitants with out-lots. Iris Island contains about seventy acres of excellent land, the upper half of which might be covered with machinery, propelled by water power; and the lower half, situated in the midst of the falls and rapids, where nature courts the imagination in her most sublime, beautiful and fascinating forms, might be converted into delightful seats for the residence of private gentlemen, or appropriated to Hotels and pleasure grounds for the accommodation of the numerous strangers who annually visit this spot. A number of manufactories, on a scale adapted to the wants of the immediate vicinity, have already been erected, and are now in successful operation at this place; among which are, a large and valuable grist mill, saw mill, two woollen cloth factories, two clothier's shops, several carding and spinning machines, a forge, paper mill, &c.

The subscribers would sell the whole of their property at this place (with the exception of the farm and private buildings of one of the proprietors) together: or they would divide it into several parts, and appropriate to each any desired number of water privileges. They would, however, be most gratified by seeing it in the hands of a single company, in which they would be glad to be interested themselves to the extent of their means. Such a company, with a commanding capital, and under a well organized and efficient administration of its concerns, might build up an establishment which would successfully compete with any thing of the kind in the United States; and would be, at once, highly useful and creditable to the country, and lucrative to themselves. The manufacture of woollen, cotten and linen goods, on an extensive scale—of iron, in all its numerous and extended ramifications; and of bread stuffs, might be undertaken to great advantage. The lake country is celebrated for the best and most abundant crops of wheat. An inexhaustible mine of iron ore, of the best quality, has lately been discovered on the margin of Lake Erie. The whole country abounds in wool; Hemp and flax grow in great luxuriance, and cotten might, at present, be introduced at a moderate expence of transportation, through the Atlantic and the Erie canal; and, at no distant day, still cheaper, through the Mississippi and the Ohio canals. The general deficiency of water power that exists along the country of the lakes—the increasing, and, already immense, population which surrounds them—their remoteness from the Atlantic ports; and the profusion and cheapness of stock and provisions, are circumstances calculated to give to this place a decided advantage over similar establishments in the eastern states, in a competition with European manufacturers. The inadequacy of capital in this part of the country to undertakings of this kind, added to the doubts which have, until very recently, existed in regard to the success of American manufactures generally, have hitherto prevented the improvements which this situation so powerfully invites. The title to the property is unquestionable, having been derived immediately from the state of New-York.

Any information, connected with the subjects of this advertisement, will be cheerfully given by Augustus Porter, who resides at the Falls, or by Peter B. Poter, at Black Rock.

Aug's Porter,
P. B. Porter.

June 24th, 1825.

B. Ferguson, Printer—Black Rock.

LITH OF WM. ENDICOTT & CO. N.Y. C.G. CREHEN.

AUGUSTUS PORTER.

B

C

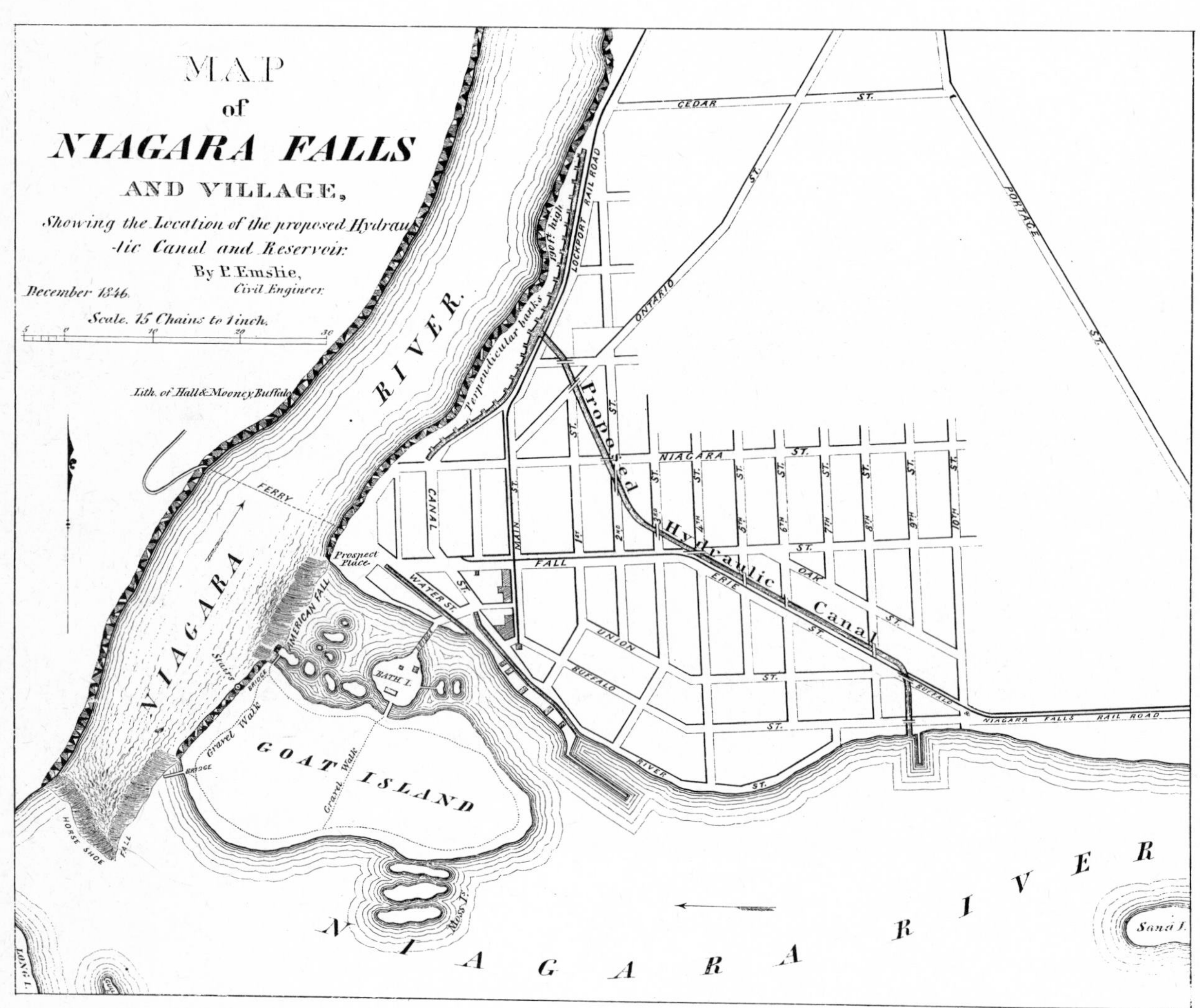
MAP
of
NIAGARA FALLS
AND VILLAGE,
Showing the Location of the proposed Hydrau-tic Canal and Reservoir.
By P. Emslie,
Civil Engineer.
December 1846.
Scale. 15 Chains to 1 inch.
Lith. of Hall & Mooney, Buffalo.
NIAGARA RIVER.
NIAGARA RIVER
GOAT ISLAND
BATH I.
AMERICAN FALL
HORSE SHOE FALL
Prospect Place
Proposed Hydraulic Canal
CEDAR ST.
ONTARIO ST.
PORTAGE ST.
NIAGARA ST.
FALL ST.
ERIE ST.
UNION
BUFFALO
RIVER ST.
MAIN ST.
CANAL
WATER ST.
OAK ST.
LOCKPORT RAIL ROAD
NIAGARA FALLS RAIL ROAD
FERRY
Gravel Walk
Sand I.

E

F

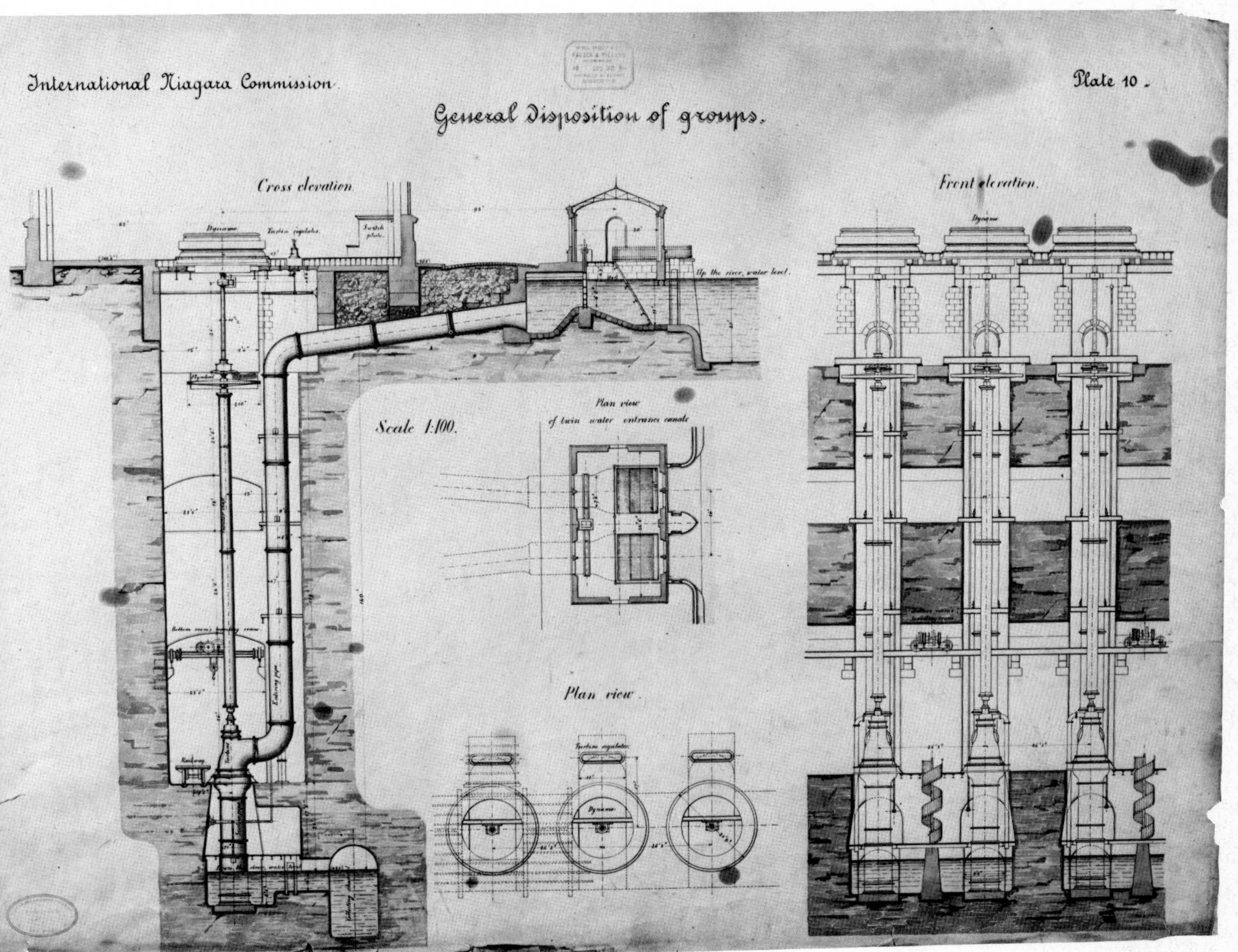
International Niagara Commission
Plate 10.
General Disposition of groups.
Cross elevation.
Front elevation.
Scale 1:100.
Plan view
of twin water entrance canals
Plan view.
Up the river, water level.
Dynamo
Turbine regulator
Switch plate
Flywheel
Delivery pipe
Tail-race

G

H

I

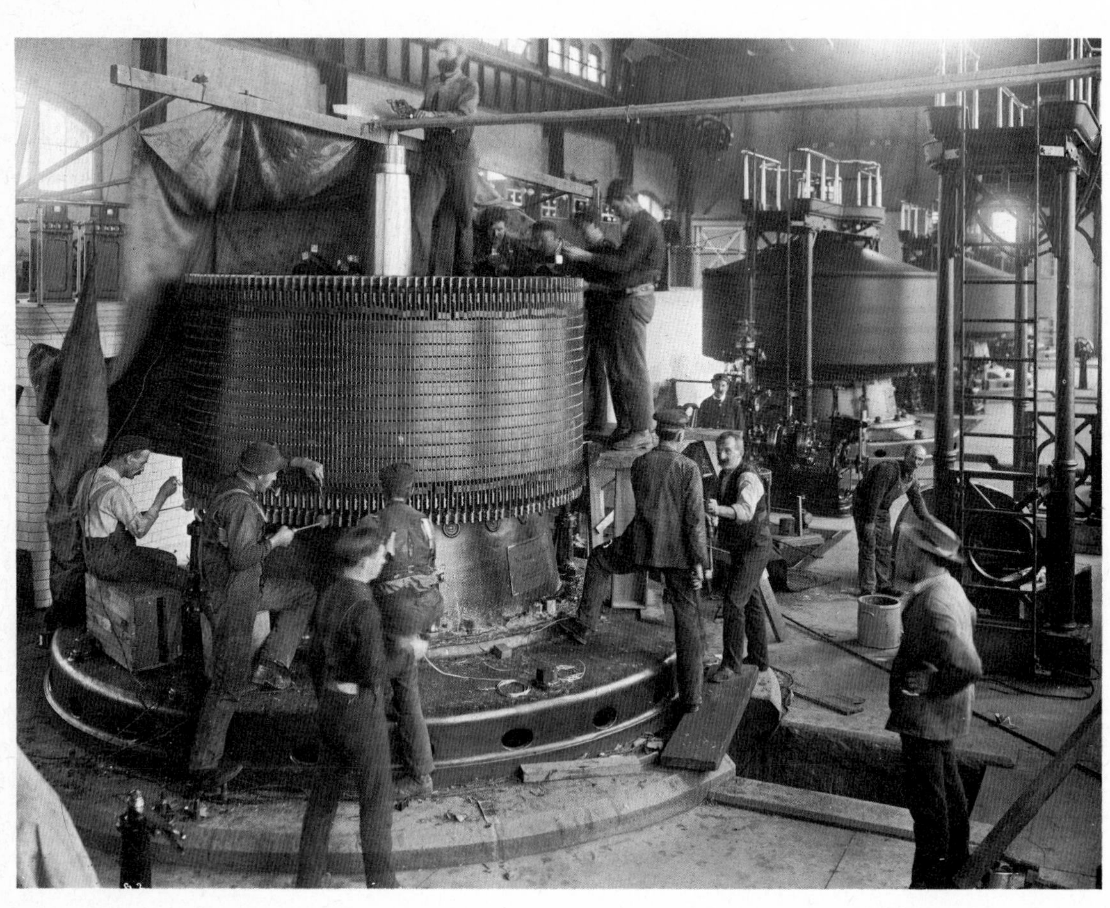

J

K

PAN-AMERICAN
EXPOSITION.
NIAGARA
BUFFALO
MAY 1 – NOVEMBER 1
1901.

L

SELECTED BIBLIOGRAPHY & INDEX

The main purpose of this selected bibliography is to list those books and documents from which quotations have been taken. Also included are a few books, mostly published since 1900, which we found to be invaluable.

GENERAL

DOW, CHARLES MASON

Anthology and bibliography of Niagara Falls. 2 vols. Albany: State of New York, 1921.

HOLDER, THOMAS

A complete record of Niagara Falls and vicinage being descriptive, historical and and industrial; containing a complete guide book, local history, manufacturing facilities, biographical sketches, business firms, etc. Niagara Falls, N.Y.: Thomas Holder, 1882.

HULBERT, ARCHER BUTLER

The Niagara River. New York and London: G. P. Putnam's Sons, 1908.

PORTER, PETER AUGUSTUS

Official guide – Niagara Falls, River, frontier – scenic, botanic, electric, historic, geologic, hydraulic. [1901.]

ALEXANDER, SIR JAMES EDWARD

Transatlantic sketches, comprising visits to the most interesting scenes in North and South America, and the West Indies. 2 vols. London: Richard Bentley, 1833.

[BIRD, ISABELLA LUCY]

The Englishwoman in America. London: John Murray, 1856.

Burke's descriptive guide; or The visitors' companion to Niagara Falls: its strange and wonderful localities. Buffalo: Andrew Burke, 1851.

CARVER, JONATHAN

Travels through the interior parts of North-America, in the years 1766, 1767, and 1768. Dublin: S. Price, R. Cross, W. Watson ..., 1779.

CHARLEVOIX, PIERRE FRANÇOIS XAVIER DE

Journal of a voyage to North-America. Undertaken by order of the French King. Containing the geographical description and natural history of the country, particularly Canada... 2 vols. London: R. and J. Dodsley, 1761.

HENNEPIN, LOUIS

A description of Louisiana. Translated from the edition of 1683 by John Gilmary Shea. New York: privately printed, 1880.

A new discovery of a vast country in America, extending above four thousand miles between New France and New Mexico... London: M. Bentley, J. Tonson, H. Bonwick, T. Goodwin, and S. Manship, 1698.

HOWELLS, WILLIAM DEAN

'Niagara, first and last.' *The Niagara book.* Buffalo: Underhill and Nichols, 1893.

JAMESON, ANNA BROWNELL (MURPHY)

Winter studies and summer rambles in Canada. 3 vols. London: Saunders & Otley, 1838.

KALM, PETER

'A letter from Mr Kalm, a Gentleman of Sweden, now on his Travels in America, to his Friend in Philadelphia; containing a particular Account of the Gr[e]at Fall of Niagara, September 2, 1750.' *The Gentleman's Magazine* (London), January 1751.

LAHONTAN, LOUIS ARMAND DE LOM D'ARCE, BARON DE

New voyages to North-America, by the Baron de Lahontan. Reprinted from the English edition of 1703, with ... introduction, notes, and index by Reuben Gold Thwaites. 2 vols. Chicago: A. C. McClurg, 1905.

MOORE, THOMAS

See DOW (General).

PORTER, COLONEL PETER A.

See DOW (General).

POWER, TYRONE

Impressions of America, during the years 1833, 1834, and 1835. 2 vols. Philadelphia: Carey, Lea & Blanchard, 1836.

FRONTIER

BABCOCK, LOUIS LOCKE

The War of 1812 on the Niagara frontier. Buffalo: Buffalo Historical Society, 1927.

DELAFIELD, JOSEPH

The unfortified boundary, a diary of the first survey of the Canadian boundary line from St. Regis to the Lake of the Woods. New York: privately printed, 1943.

DE VEAUX, SAMUEL

The falls of Niagara, or Tourist's guide to this wonder of nature, including notices of the whirlpool, islands, &c., and a complete guide thro' the Canadas. Buffalo: William B. Hayden, 1839.

GAUUST, DOSCEN, *pseud.*

History of the Fenian invasion of Canada. Hamilton, C.W.: Wm. Brown & Co.

LEVINGE, SIR RICHARD GEORGE AUGUSTUS

Echoes from the backwoods; or Sketches of transatlantic life. 2 vols. London: Henry Colburn, 1846.

O'CALLAGHAN, EDMUND BAILEY

The documentary history of the State of New York. 4 vols. Albany: Weed, Parsons, & Co., 1849-50.

POUCHOT, PIERRE

Memoir upon the late war in North America, between the French and English, 1755-60; followed by observations upon the theatre of actual war.... Translated and edited by Franklin B. Hough. 2 vols. Roxbury, Mass.: W. Elliot Woodward, 1866.

SEVERANCE, FRANK HAYWARD

An old frontier of France, the Niagara region and adjacent lakes under French control. 2 vols. New York: Dodd, Mead, and Company, 1917.

TIFFANY, ORRIN EDWARD

'The relations of the United States to the Canadian rebellion of 1837-1838.' *Publications of the Buffalo Historical Society*, vol. VIII. Buffalo, 1905.

EXPANSION

BUCK, LEFFERT L.

Report on the renewal of Niagara Suspension Bridge. 1880. New York: C. W. Ames & Co., 1881.

[D'ARUSMONT, FRANCES (WRIGHT)]

Views of society and manners in America... By an Englishwoman. London: Longman, Hurst, Rees, Orme, and Brown, 1821.

HOWISON, JOHN

Sketches of Upper Canada, domestic, local and characteristic... Edinburgh: Oliver & Boyd; London: G. & W. B. Whittaker, 1821.

ROEBLING, JOHN AUGUSTUS

Final report of John A. Roebling, civil engineer, to the presidents and directors of the Niagara Falls Suspension and Niagara Falls International Bridge Companies. May 1, 1855. Second edition. Albion, N.Y.: A. M. Eddy, 1892.

TROUT, JOHN MALCOLM and EDWARD

The railways of Canada for 1870-1... Toronto: The Monetary Times, 1871.

YATES, RAYMOND F.

The old Lockport and Niagara Falls strap railroad. Lockport, N.Y.: Niagara County Historical Society, 1950.

STUNTERS

See General.

TOURISTS

DELAFIELD, JOSEPH

See p. 175.

The fashionable tour; or A trip to the Springs, Niagara, Quebeck, and Boston, in the summer of 1821. Saratoga Springs, N.Y.: G. M. Davison, 1822.

HARRISON, JONATHAN BAXTER

The condition of Niagara Falls, and the measures needed to preserve them.... New York: privately printed, 1882.

HILL, ROWLAND F.

Letter of Rowland F. Hill in opposition to the international park or state reservation at Niagara Falls. New York: privately printed, 1881.

JOHNSON, F. H.

Guide to Niagara Falls and its scenery, including all the points of interest both on the American and Canadian side. Philadelphia: George W. Childs, 1864.

KINGSTON, WILLIAM HENRY GILES

Western wanderings or, a pleasure tour in the Canadas. 2 vols. London: Chapman and Hall, 1856.

LEVINGE, SIR RICHARD GEORGE AUGUSTUS

See p. 175.

'The Ordnance Chain Reserve at Niagara Falls.' Series A-7, Record Group 1, Crown Lands Dept. (This collection of papers in the Ontario Archives contains the report of E. B. Wood and copies of other documents regarding the abuses on the Canadian side of the Falls.)

[PORTER, ALBERT HOWELL]

Historical sketch of Niagara from 1678 to 1876. Privately printed.

Report of the Commissioners of the State Reservation at Niagara for the year 1885.

ROLPH, THOMAS

A brief account together with observations, made during a visit in the West Indies, and a tour through the United States of America, in parts of the years 1832-3; together with a statistical account of Upper Canada. Dundas, U.C.: G. Heyworth Hackstaff, 1836.

SCHULTZ, CHRISTIAN

Travels on an inland voyage through the states of New York, Pennsylvania, Virginia, Ohio, Kentucky and Tennessee, and through the territories of Indiana, Louisiana, Mississippi and New-Orleans; performed in the years 1807 and 1808; including a tour of nearly six thousand miles. 2 vols. New York: Isaac Riley, 1810.

[SEARS, EDWARD S.]

Faxon's illustrated handbook of travel to Saratoga, Lakes George and Champlain, the Adirondacks, Niagara Falls, Montreal, Quebec, the Saguenay River, the White Mountains, Lakes Memphremagog and Winnipiseogee. Revised edition, 1874. Boston: C. A. Faxon [1874].

SMITH, WILLIAM HENRY

Smith's Canadian gazetteer; comprising statistical and general information respecting all parts of the upper province, or Canada West. Toronto: H. & W. Rowsell, 1846.

Special report of New York State Survey on the preservation of the scenery of Niagara Falls. Albany: Charles Van Benthuysen & Sons, 1880.

STREET, SAMUEL

Papers. (Ontario Archives.)

Tenth annual report of the Commissioners for the Queen Victoria Niagara Falls Park, 1895. Toronto: Warwick Bros. & Rutter, 1896.

TROLLOPE, ANTHONY

North America. 2 vols. Philadelphia: J. B. Lippincott, 1862.

[WARBURTON, GEORGE DROUGHT]

Hochelaga; or, England in the New World. Edited by Eliot Warburton. Second edition, revised. London: Henry Colburn, 1846.

WATERTON, CHARLES

Wanderings in South America, the northwest of the United States, and the Antilles in the years 1812, 1816, 1820, and 1824. Second edition. London: B. Fellowes, 1828.

WELD, CHARLES RICHARD

A vacation tour in the United States and Canada. London: Longman, Brown, Green, and Longmans, 1855.

WERGE, JOHN

The evolution of photography... London: Piper & Carter, and John Werge, 1890.

WOODS, NICHOLAS AUGUSTUS

The Prince of Wales in Canada and the United States. London: Bradbury & Evans, 1861.

POWER

ADAMS, EDWARD DEAN

Niagara power; history of the Niagara Falls Power Company 1886-1918; evolution of its central power station and alternating current system. 2 vols. Niagara Falls, N.Y.: privately printed for the Niagara Falls Power Company, 1927.

LEVASSEUR, AUGUSTE

Lafayette in America in 1824 and 1825; or journal of travels, in the United States. New York: White, Gallaher, & White ..., 1829.

Scientific American Supplement No. 1261; Niagara Falls industrial number. March 3, 1900.

INDEX

Abbott, Francis 5-6
Adams, Edward Dean 156
Adams Power Station 158-9
Alexander, Sir James Edward *q* 5-6
  watercolour by *Image* K

Babbitt, Platt D. 112
  photographs by *Stunters* D, H, I, *Tourists* E, I, M, N
Barnett, Thomas 124
Bath Island 116, 117, 121, *Tourists* A, T, 161
Beachey, Lincoln 87, *Stunters* R
Bellini, Henry 84-5, *Stunters* K
Bird, Isabella Lucy 6
Blondin (Jean François Gravelet) 82-3, 84, *Stunters* C, D, E, G, 113
Bornet, John 7
  lithograph by *Image* H
Bridges
  Cantilever (Michigan Central) 66, *Expansion* M
  Ellet's Suspension 61, 113
  Lower Steel Arch (Whirlpool Rapids) 64, *Expansion* M
  Queenston-Lewiston (proposed) 60, *Expansion* F
  Roebling's Railway Suspension 61-4, *Expansion* H, I, L
  Upper Steel Arch (Falls View) *Stunters* R, 162, *Power* F
  Upper Suspension 111, 162
Brock, Major-General Sir Isaac 28-9, 37, *Frontier* H
  monument 34
Butler, Lieutenant-Colonel John 27
  Butler's Barracks 28
  Butler's Rangers 27, 28

Canals
  Erie 58, 59, 60, 64, *Expansion* A, 153
  'Hydraulic' 154, 162, *Power* D
  Proposed American Ship 58-9, *Expansion* E
  Welland 58, 59
Caroline 33, *Frontier* M, N
Carver, Captain Jonathan *q* 3-4
Cataract Construction Company 156, 158
Cave of the Winds 122
Chain reserve 110, 115, 118
Charlevoix, Pierre François Xavier de *q* 2-3
Church, Frederick Edwin 6-7
'City of the Falls' 110
Clark, Thomas 111

Davies, Lieutenant Thomas 3
  painting by *Image* D
Delafield, Major Joseph *q* 32, 109
Denonville, Marquis de 25, 26
De Veaux, Samuel *q* 27-8
Devil's Hole Massacre 27
Dongan, Colonel Thomas 25, 26
Drew, Captain Andrew 33
Dufferin, Lord 116, 117

Edison, Thomas A. 157-8
Ellet, Charles 61
Emslie, Peter 154
  map by *Power* D
England, William 123
  photographs by *Expansion* H, I, *Tourists* K, P

Evershed, Thomas 155, 156, 158

Faesch & Piccard 157
plan by *Power* S
Farini (William Leonard Hunt) 83-4, 90, *Stunters* H, I
Faxon's *Illustrated handbook of travel* *q* 115-16
Ferry 110, 111, 125, *Tourists* G
Flack, Robert 86
Forsyth, William 82, 110
Fort Conti 25, 26
Fort Erie 27, 31, *Frontier* D, K
Fort George 28, 31, *Frontier* C
Fort Niagara 25-8, *Frontier* A, B
Fort Schlosser 27

Gardner, James T. 116-17, 118, 119
Gaskill, Charles B. 154, 156
Gauust, Doscen (pseud.) *q* 35
Goat Island 8, 32, 115, 116
Graham, Carlisle D. 86, 87, *Stunters* O

Hackstaff, George H. vi
Harrison, J. B. *q* 117
Height of Falls 2-3
Hennepin, Father Louis 1-3
'Hermit of Niagara' 5-6
Hill, Rowland F. *q* 117
Hooker, Samuel 121, *Tourists* A
Hotels
Cataract House 109, 122, *Tourists* D, E
Clifton House 121, *Tourists* B, C
Eagle Tavern 109
International 122, *Tourists* E
Pavilion 110
Howells, W. D. *q* 6, 7
Howison, John *q* 57
Hulbert, Archer Butler *q* 87

Ice Bridge 7, 127, *Tourists* Y
Incline Railway 125, *Tourists* R, S
International Carnival (1911) 87, *Stunters* S
International Niagara Commission 156-7, 158

Jameson, Anna *q* 6, 7
Jenkins, 'Professor' 84, *Stunters* J
Johnson, Sir William 26, 27

Kalm, Peter *q* 2-3
Kingston, W. H. G. *q* 111

Lahontan, Baron de *q* 2
Levasseur, Auguste *q* 153
Levinge, Sir Richard G. A. *q* 34, 112
engraving after *Frontier* F
Lundy's Lane 31, 111

Mackenzie, William Lyon 32-4, 81-2
'Maid of the Mist' 6
Maid of the Mist (steamer) 83, 84, 113-14, *Tourists* P
Manchester (Niagara Falls) 109, 153
Mason, Samuel 112, *Tourists* L
Merritt, William Hamilton 58, 60
Michigan 81-2, *Stunters* A
Moore, Thomas *q* 4

Navy Island 33, 112
Newark (Niagara) 28, 31
Niagara Falls Canal Company 154
Niagara Falls Hydraulic Company 154
Niagara Falls Hydraulic Power and Manufacturing Company 154, 162
Niagara Falls International Bridge Company 60
Niagara Falls Paper Manufacturing Company 161
Niagara Falls Power Company 156, 158
Niagara Falls Suspension Bridge Company 60
Niagara Falls Water Power Company 154
Niagara River Hydraulic Tunnel, Power and Sewer Company 155-6

Olmsted, Frederick Law 116, 118, 119
O'Neill, 'General' John 34-5

Pagoda, The 114
Pan-American Exposition 159, *Power* L
Patch, Sam 82, *Stunters* B
Peer, Stephen 85, 86, *Stunters* L
Photography 7, 112, 115, 123, *Tourists* L
Pierie, Lieutenant William 3
Pittsburgh Reduction Company (Aluminum Company of America) 158, 162
Portage, Niagara 25, 27, 57-8
Porter, Augustus 58, 109, 153-4, *Power* B
Porter, Barton & Company 58, *Expansion* B
Porter, Colonel Peter A. *q* 7-8
Porter, Peter A. *q* 113
Porter, General Peter B. 30, 58, *Frontier* J, 116, 153-4
Porter's Mills 161, *Power* C
Pouchot, Captain Pierre *q* 26-7
Power, Tyrone *q* 4-5
Prince of Wales (Edward VII) 112-13, *Tourists* M
Prospect Park 115-16, 117, 155
Prospect Point 112, 115-16

Queenston Heights, battle of 29, *Frontier* E
Queen Victoria Park 118, 126

Railroads or Railways
Buffalo & Niagara Falls 59, *Expansion* G
Canandaigua & Niagara Falls 62-3
Erie & Ontario 60, 61, *Expansion* J
Great Western 61, 62, 63, 64, 123, *Tourists* K
Lockport & Niagara Falls 59-60
Michigan Central 61, 66, *Expansion* M
New York Central 60, 61, 62, 63, 126
Niagara Falls Park & River 126, *Tourists* X
Niagara Gorge 126

Robinson, Joel R. 113
Robinson, Governor Lucius 116
Roebling, John Augustus 61-4, *Expansion* K
Rolph, Thomas *q* 114
Russian Naval Officers, visit of 124, *Tourists* N

Schoellkopf, Arthur 155
Schoellkopf, Jacob F. 154
Schoellkopf Power Station 162
Schultz, Christian *q* 109
Scott, Major-General Winfield 29, 31, 33, 34, *Frontier* I
Sellers, Coleman 156, 157
Shadow of the Rock 125, *Tourists* Q, R
Sheaffe, Major-General Sir Roger Hale 29
Smith, W. H. *q* 111-12
Smyth, Brigadier-General Alexander 29-30
  proclamation by *Frontier* F
Spelterini, Maria 85-6, *Stunters* M, N
State Reservation 117, *Tourists* V
Stedman, John 27, 58
Street, Samuel 111
Sult, Stephen *q* 59-60

Table Rock 9, *Image* F, K, 82, 122
Table Rock House 114-15
Taylor, Anna Edson 86, *Stunters* Q
Termination Rock 4, 122, *Tourists* F, H
Terrapin Tower 6-7, *Image* I, L, 111
Thomson, James 112
Thomson, Sir William (Lord Kelvin) 156, 157
Trollope, Anthony *q* 111
Tugby's Bazaar 126, *Tourists* W

Van Rensselaer, Rensselaer 33, 34
Van Rensselaer, Major-General Stephen 29

Walsh, Lieutenant Edward 37
  watercolours by *Frontier* C, D
Warburton, G. D. *q* 114
Waterton, Charles *q* 109-10
Webb, Captain Matthew 86, *Stunters* P
Welch, Thomas V. *q* 118
Weld, Charles Richard *q* 112
Werge, John *q* 112
Westinghouse, George 157, 158
Whitney, Parkhurst 109, 110
Willard, Maud 86
Wood, E. B. *q* 115
Woods, Nicholas A. *q* 113
Wright, Frances (D'Arusmont) *q* 57